Reasons to Be Glad

Reasons to Be Glad

A Collection of Excellent Reading
From "Decision" Magazine, Compiled by the Editors

Reasons to Be Glad

©1988 Billy Graham Evangelistic Association.

World Wide Publications is the publishing ministry of the Billy Graham Evangelistic Association.

Scripture quotations at the beginning of the chapters are taken from The Holy Bible, New International Version, copyright ©1973, 1978, 1984 International Bible Society. Used by permission of Zondervan Bible publishers.

Library of Congress Catalog Card Number: 88-51051

ISBN 0-89066-138-3

Cover Photo: ©1986 Jerry Bushey

Printed in U.S.A.

Table of Contents

Introduction

Reasons to Be Glad

We hear you!

Again and again, as we open our mail each day, we find letters asking: "Will you send a copy of an article I read last year about . . ." Or, "I save 'Decision' because there is so much in its pages worth rereading." Or, "I wish I could get a collection of the best of 'Decision.' "

In 1983 we published a collection of 98 "Decision" articles in the book titled "Wondrous Power, Wondrous Love." Since that time, a wealth of excellent material has been printed in the magazine. So we decided once again to select what we considered to be some of the best and most popular articles and compile them in the book you now hold in your hands.

Here are stories about people that will tug at your heart and cause you to rejoice at the way God meets us in our everyday lives. Here are quality teaching articles, biblical studies, inspirational pieces and messages by leading Christians, including Billy Graham. We believe that this book will help you grow in your relationship with Jesus Christ and in your personal witness.

As you open these pages and begin to read, we think you will find such a rich storehouse of good things that it will be hard to put the book down. And we think you will say, "I have several friends who are looking for a book just like this one."

Compiling this collection was a great pleasure for us. We pray that you will find yourself saying, "Look at what God is doing in the lives of trusting people; look at the blessing and the promises and the reasons for praise." When that happens, we will be glad.

—The Editors of "Decision"

1

Knowing God Today

"I consider everything a loss compared to the surpassing greatness of knowing Christ Jesus my Lord."
Philippians 3:8

The Wake-Up Call

Gwen Lam

Well!" exclaimed my boss. "You've certainly changed. I can
remember a time when you would hit the ceiling over the
kind of things that were said in that meeting . . . "

As he happily reviewed the meeting, I sent a silent prayer of
thanks to God. I was grateful for two things. First, that God was
teaching me patience, especially in listening more carefully to other
points of view and in raising opposing points in a more open, con-
ciliatory manner.

Second, that my colleague had noted a difference in my behavior.
He was right; there had indeed been a time when I was the ready
antagonist, marshalling facts to shoot down ideas at odds with my
own. Fortunately, the Lord was changing me.

The seeds for this change were planted back in the 1970s, during a period when I was experiencing a desire to know God better. An unexpected letter from an older brother prompted the
dramatic breakthrough. To my astonishment and dismay, his letter announced that he had enrolled me in a 16-week Bible memory

Gwen Lam is vice president of an education consultant firm in New York City
and has written and edited a variety of educational materials. She lives in New
York City and attends Fifth Avenue Presbyterian Church. ©1983 Gwen Lam.

course. How thankful I am that the Holy Spirit stopped me from following my initial inclination—to write back with thanks, saying a heavy schedule prevented my taking on anything else. A voice within whispered, "If he loves you enough to take the trouble and even pay the fee, hadn't you better find the time?"

I found the time and Scripture began to find me. One verse, in fact, kept bubbling into my consciousness at odd moments—when I was walking along the street, riding the bus, participating in a business conference, listening to a sermon. One night, as I was in bed reading, the verse interrupted again.

"The Lord God hath given me the tongue of the learned, that I should know how to speak a word in season to him that is weary: he wakeneth morning by morning, he wakeneth mine ear to hear as the learned."[1]

I closed the book, sat up in bed and said, "Lord, You seem to be trying to get my attention with this verse. Are You saying You want me to get up earlier in the morning so that You will have more time to teach me? You want more than the 15 or 20 minutes I give You now? If so, You wake me whenever You want."

The next morning, with no alarm set, I awakened exactly one hour ahead of my usual getting-up time. I felt clearheaded and refreshed. When I gave God the extra hour he requested and asked him to direct its use, my personality and performance began to change. The growth has been gradual, of course, and is still under way.

For many years my devotional life had lacked firm direction and clarity of purpose. During some periods I dutifully worked my way through a book of the Bible, but I didn't get much from it. My brief unstructured prayers included thanksgiving and requests for general "blessings" on people and situations that I cared about. Crisis situations sent me into more fervent prayer, but mostly I just checked in with God.

With the luxury of "an hour plus" of quality morning time, I have made two significant changes in my devotions. These involve the approach to devotional Bible study and the structure and content of morning prayers.

I now read Scripture in an organized, action-oriented fashion, taking a short portion and asking the Holy Spirit to help me understand what it says and apply it to my own life. Sometimes the message comforts, provides help for a specific problem or just gives fresh evidence of the awesome power and love of God. Sometimes the message speaks directly to a fault I need to correct.

With the new procedure, Bible reading passed quickly from being an unfulfilling duty to an activity I now approach expectantly, eager to see what he will teach me each day.

As I study and meditate on a passage, I also ask the Lord to highlight a special verse—just for me. I copy the verse in the spiritual journal I keep, noting what it says to me and how I will act on it. Recently I began underlining those verses in red, and sometimes I copy them on cards to read on the bus or subway.

One journal entry illustrates how devotional Bible study works for me. On a Wednesday in February I read Ephesians 5:8-16 in which Paul urged Christians to walk as children of light, emerging from the darkness that formerly enveloped them. My verse: "[Try] to learn what is pleasing to the Lord."[2]

"This is my goal," notes my journal, "to learn what it is that pleases him. And then do it! I am thankful the way to learn has been clarified for me by the Holy Spirit. My goal is getting into his Word and letting it speak to me. And being still, cultivating a receptive mind and heart that his message may take root and bear fruit. This day, may I begin a habit of testing every response to each perplexing situation with the basic question, 'Will my action be pleasing to him?' "

The prayer of my quiet time comes after Scripture exploration. This went through the same metamorphosis as Bible study. I didn't know how to go about it and had great difficulty keeping my mind harnessed to the task. I felt I was failing as a Christian because prayer time didn't bring the joy and sense of spiritual movement that Scripture study produced.

The Holy Spirit answered my cry for prayer help by assigning me to apprentice Grethe Anderson during the last year of her life. Grethe, a radiant missionary, had just been appointed superintendent of the Women's Bible Society of New York. When she learned I was a writer, she asked if I would help her develop a visual presentation of dedicated Christian women who had advanced the Kingdom of God in the city of New York in the 1800s. It was a faith-deepening experience for me.

As I worked with Grethe, I learned much about the practice of prayer. She preceded each step with a request for God's guidance and wisdom, and she thanked him in advance for his help and at the end for his faithfulness.

I didn't, however, tumble to the notion that the same prayer procedure could be applied to my secular work until I experienced the follow-through by Grethe and God to a small problem I posed to her.

It happened one day when I stopped at her office to pick her up for lunch and give her a progress report. As she assembled papers to take along, I talked happily about the way the presentation was taking shape.

"We've got a wonderful story, Grethe," I said. "I wish I had time to go after one more bit of information. I don't really need it, but I wish I had time to go to the library and find out more about what New York City was like in 1815. But I've run out of time and . . ."

"God can handle that little detail," she said. "We'll pray about it before we go to lunch."

A few minutes later in the elevator we were joined by the archivist of the American Bible Society (ABS). Her face brightened when she saw us. "I'm so glad I ran into you," she said. "I came across two essays you might find useful. One is a profile of New York City in 1815 when the ABS and the Women's Society were formed. The other is on the religious situation here at the time."

Later, as I pondered not only the instant answer to prayer but Grethe's calm assurance of God's concern for every small detail of our project, I began to realize what real faith and trust were all about. And I also began to sense the Lord inviting me to pray about my secular work and the ordinary events of daily life. I accepted that invitation.

I still have a long way to go in my spiritual growth. With Paul I am quick to say, "I do not regard myself as having laid hold of it yet."[3] I still slip back into the old ways. Impatience and pride surface too often. When this happens, I turn to the seventh chapter of Romans and find comfort in the fact that Paul also struggled mightily with two conflicting natures. And I too press on, claiming the power of Christ within to produce victory. It is during my morning quiet time that I am filled with a fresh, abundant supply of that power.

(1) Isaiah 50:4, KJV. (2) Ephesians 5:10, NASB. (3) Philippians 3:13, NASB. Bible verses marked NASB are taken by permission from the New American Standard Bible, copyright ©1960, 1962, 1963, 1968, 1971, 1972, 1973, 1975, 1977 The Lockman Foundation, La Habra, California

The Lordship of Jesus Christ

John R. W. Stott

I believe that the master-key Christian doctrine is in the affirmation "Jesus is Lord." If we see and acknowledge Jesus as Lord, then all our Christian doctrine and behavior and experience mesh, and we have found the integrating secret of the Christian life. The Lordship of Jesus is a wonderfully liberating doctrine. It is when Jesus is Lord that we are made whole and free.

When we acknowledge Jesus as Lord, our relationship to him is right.[1] The whole of our human experience centers on Jesus Christ. If we are Christians, nothing is outside the sphere of his dominion. "To this end Christ died and lived again, that he might be . . ."[2] What? Suppose you didn't know that verse, and I said, "Fill in the blank." Ninety-nine out of 100 would say "Savior." Isn't that why he died and rose again, to be our Savior? But that is not what Paul said. He said, ". . . that he might be Lord."[2]

John Stott is president of London Institute for Contemporary Christianity and was rector of All Souls Church, Langham Place, London. He is the author of 27 books, including "The Authentic Jesus." This article is taken by permission from "The Lordship of Jesus Christ," by John R. W. Stott, in "The Gospel, the Spirit, the Church," ed. by David Porter, STL Books, Bromley, Kent, England. ©1978 The Keswick Convention Council, London.

The idea still lingers in some circles that it is possible to accept Jesus as Savior and postpone indefinitely the question of his Lordship. The New Testament knows nothing of such bogus Christianity. There is only one Jesus Christ, he is our Lord and Savior Jesus Christ; and response to Jesus is response to the totality of Jesus our Savior and Lord. He can only *be* our Savior because he *is* Lord. It is from that position at the Father's right hand that he justifies the believing sinner and bestows the Holy Spirit upon us; because he has the authority to do so.

In heaven the Christian dead give no grudging acquiescence to the Lordship of Jesus. But Jesus died and rose again not only to be Lord of the dead but of the living. Our Christian life on earth is to approximate as closely as possible the glorified life of the believer in heaven. That means totality of surrender to the Lordship of Jesus, offering him joyful, ungrudging and total allegiance.

Second, when we acknowledge Jesus as Lord, our relationship to one another is right. Do you know Romans 14? It is mostly about the "weaker brother." The weaker brother is the Christian with an underdeveloped and oversensitive conscience. In the church or churches in Rome there were Christians with a weak conscience and those with a strong conscience. Some Christians regarded some days as better and more important than others, and others regarded all days as alike.

Of course we must be agreed about the major doctrines and all the fundamentals of the faith. But there is no reason why we shouldn't differ about minor matters. We are not going to agree with one another totally until we get to heaven, so we have to learn to be tolerant of one another in the Christian family.

What disturbed the Apostle Paul was not so much the existence of differences but the attitudes the Christians had toward one another on account of their differences. They despised one another; they sat in judgment on one another.[3]

But we have no business to despise one another, no business to stand in judgment on the servants of Christ.[4] Paul would voluntarily curb his own liberty of conscience in the presence of weak brothers or sisters, because it might cause them to do something against their conscience.

The secret of our relationships with one another in the Christian Church, especially when we have differences, is "Jesus Christ is Lord." To despise or stand in judgment on a fellow Christian isn't just a breach of fellowship. It is a denial of the Lordship of

Jesus. I need to say to myself, who am I, that I should cast myself in the role of another Christian's lord and judge? I must be willing for Jesus Christ to be not only my Lord and Judge, but also my fellow Christians' Lord and Judge. They are responsible to him, and I must not interfere with Christ's Lordship over other Christians.

Third, if we acknowledge Jesus as Lord, then our relationship with the world outside is right as well; that is, the secular, the unbelieving, the Christ-rejecting world. Look to verse 11. The context here[5] is judgment. Each of us is going to give an account of himself to Christ the Lord and Christ the Judge, and we must not therefore be lords and judges of each other. Nevertheless, these words have a wider implication.

In Philippians 2:9-11 we read that God has exalted Jesus so that at his name "every knee should bow, . . . and every tongue confess that Jesus Christ is Lord."[6] So what then is the supreme missionary motivation? It is the universal Lordship of Jesus. God has exalted Jesus and enthroned him at his right hand. God has given him authority over all nations, and God's purpose in doing this is that every knee should bow to Jesus and every tongue confess him as Lord.

God has made Jesus Lord of all by creation, and also by his death and resurrection and ascension and enthronement at the right hand of God. He died and rose again that he might be Lord "both of the dead and of the living."[7] So I want to ask, did Jesus die and rise in vain?

This key doctrine, the Lordship of Jesus, is like the last piece of the jigsaw, the keystone in the arch, the final digit in the combination lock. If we acknowledge Jesus as Lord, everything else fits into place. Our relationships to him, with one another, and to the world, are put right.

Is Jesus Christ your Lord? Or are you denying his Lordship in some way? To reject his teaching, to disobey his moral commandments, to rebel against his providential will, are all to deny the Lordship of Jesus. To control other Christians, to despise or stand in judgment of fellow Christians—these are to deny the Lordship of Jesus. To do nothing about the Christian mission in areas of the world where he is not acknowledged is to deny his Lordship. And to deny the Lordship of Jesus in any respect is to set ourselves against the purpose for which he died and rose again.

Will you surrender to him what you have been withholding for years, whatever it be?

---

(1) Romans 14:7-9. (2) Romans 14:9, RSV. (3) Romans 14:2-3. (4) Romans 14:4. (5) Romans 14:10-12.
(6) Philippians 2:10-11, RSV. (7) Romans 14:9, RSV

◆ ◆ ◆

We recognize him
by the music
that goes wherever he goes . . .
grace notes
adorn the clay
of our commonplace;
clear notes of comfort
make themselves heard
in most unlikely places;
immortal melodies claim their right
to transform a wake
into a jubilee.
Oh, yes, we know him . . .
and keep listening
for the wonder;
the echoes never die,
and forever music keeps
coming back.
    —VIOLA JACOBSON BERG
      Malverne, New York

Jelly on the Bible

Glen Hale Bump

L ook out, Daddy!" warned little David at the breakfast table. "You're getting jelly on the Bible!"

It was one of the hazards of morning devotions, but we believed the payoff was well worth such minor hazards. Raising a couple of boys and working in the turbulent world of sales, advertising and public relations, I found that risking a little jelly on the Bible at breakfast kept me from getting egg on my face throughout the day!

Our family crises were mostly minor. No divorce, drugs or crime. We had only the loss of two good jobs, two major residence moves, the usual children's health and personality problems, and increasing responsibilities regarding aging relatives. God has handily solved these things for us and, I am convinced, has prevented them from causing major upsets in our lives. One reason is certainly the daily family devotions which helped keep us calm in potentially explosive situations. People with serious difficulties have told us how fami-

---

Glen Hale Bump is a free-lance writer. He has written numerous articles and a book titled "How to Succeed in Business Without Being a Pagan." He and his wife, Frances, are the parents of two sons and live in Orlando, Florida. They attend Downtown Baptist Church in Orlando. ©1987 Glen Hale Bump.

ly devotions have kept them from going to pieces too.

We learned that daily time with God guards the gearbox of our daily grind from the devil's sand of discouragement, anger, frustration and fear. We read in the Psalms, "Early will I seek thee,"[1] and then the result: "Thy right hand upholdeth me."[2] In Proverbs we read: "Those that seek me early shall find me,"[3] and again in the Psalms: "Thy word is a lamp unto my feet, and a light unto my path."[4]

How? His Word gives personal guidance and teaches love and concern for others. It feeds our spirits and minds; it helps us think straight. Neither Sunday school nor church alone can do it. Character and citizenship strong enough to resist moral disease start at home in devotions where little problems can stop before they get big.

We've learned that we can't read the Bible and pray for each other when we're angry or hurt. Prayer time is a time to say, "I'm sorry," or, "I love you," or, "I have a problem." It's a time to speak in love, gently and sincerely, with a willingness to listen to the other person's side of the story and forgive if anyone feels he has been wronged. When one shares a problem, the others assure him that they will be praying for him that day.

Bible reading and prayer give a spiritual boost to go out strong against hurts, frustrations, fears and temptations. We're powered by the Source of all power, the Power who built the earth and everything in space, the Power who controls it all! Paul said, "If God be for us, who can be against us?"[5] With that in our heads we can overcome failed exams, a stock market crash, the loss of a job or a tournament championship.

It doesn't take long to read a few Bible verses and have each person pray. Scripture promises: "If my people, which are called by my name, shall humble themselves, and pray, and seek my face, and turn from their wicked ways; then will I hear from heaven, and will forgive their sin, and will heal their land."[6]

The Bible says "Fear not." David, the youngest of our family, had many fears, not realizing that all of us have had the same fears too. He needed reassurance during his first few years. Daily devotions helped teach him where help could be found. Once on a trip we became lost on a back road that ended in a swamp. As I carefully turned the car around on the remnant of road, we seemed suddenly to be practically in the water. David peered over the back seat and, with his voice quivering, asked, "God is looking out for us, isn't he?"

Perhaps "Fear not" is an easier lesson to teach a child than "Do good to them that hate you, and pray for them which despitefully use you, and persecute you."[7] We helped Richard learn this principle when he was victimized by a bully. Our adjustment to life depends so much on our attitude! Praying for enemies helps turn our hatred to pity which can be the first step toward love.

"Wouldn't you hate to be like that person?" we asked our son.

"Yes!"

"Don't you feel sorry for anybody like that?"

"Yes."

So we prayed together that the bully would escape his mean self so that people wouldn't hate him. This concept of pity made us realize that all bullies in life—children or adults—are prisoners of personality problems which probably cause them to act the way they do.

Because our family had a need for daily devotions, our getting-up time was 10 or 15 minutes earlier to allow for that. Right after breakfast we read Scripture and the devotional thought, if there was one, and then we prayed, one person at a time, for personal or family problems or both. We prayed for relatives, friends, business or school associates, government authorities—whoever—as need indicated and time allowed. No holy language was necessary. We just said it. We thanked God for things, asked him for health, money, guidance, forgiveness—whatever. We listened carefully to our children's prayers. We found that deeply hidden needs surfaced, giving us a chance to ward off serious trouble later by discussing after prayer time some problem that was urgent right then.

We accept the miracle of breakfast turning into energy, and we accept the miracle of biblical nourishment becoming emotional and spiritual energy to power us through daily difficulties and make us helpful to others. We never minded a little jelly on the Bible.

---

(1) Psalm 63:1, KJV. (2) Psalm 63:8, KJV. (3) Proverbs 8:17, KJV. (4) Psalm 119:105, KJV. (5) Romans 8:31, KJV. (6) 2 Chronicles 7:14, KJV. (7) Matthew 5:44, KJV

The Holy Spirit in Our Lives

Maurice Wood

To visualize God the Father is easy because we have an idea of fatherhood. It is wonderfully simple to think of God the Son, because again we have so much we can use our imaginations to think about. But to imagine God the Holy Spirit is not so easy. And yet, the more one studies the Scriptures about the Holy Spirit, the more one comes to rejoice in the truth and fact of the Third Person of the Trinity.

Much of the work of the Holy Spirit is something which we hardly realize is going on. So much of it is his own gentle, loving, protecting but unseen work. We do not know always that God has saved us from some physical problem, from some mental distress, perhaps from some moral blunder, by the unseen hand of the Holy Spirit caring for us. But Scripture is definite about great truths and affirmations concerning the Holy Spirit.

Maurice Wood, D.S.C., M.A., R.N.R., is a bishop of the Church of England and the chairman of the Order of Christian Unity. He and his wife, Margaret, have six grown children. They make their home in Englefield, Near Reading, England. This article is taken by permission from "The Holy Spirit in the Life of the Christian," by M.A.P. Wood, in "The Keswick Week 1968," ©1968 The Keswick Convention Council; Marshall, Morgan and Scott, Ltd., Basingstoke, Hants, England.

The Holy Spirit and the Scriptures

I wonder if you have ever said, "I wish I'd seen Jesus with my own eyes. I wish I'd heard him speak by Galilee. I wish I'd gazed upon the cross and seen him loving me enough to die for me. I wish I'd looked into the empty tomb and found that he was alive again; and I wish I'd watched him ascend to heaven, to the very right hand of God himself on the throne."

This is what the Holy Spirit desires to do for us, in and through the Holy Scriptures: "I will pray the Father, and he shall give you another Comforter, that he may abide with you for ever; Even the Spirit of truth; whom the world cannot receive, because it seeth him not, neither knoweth him: but ye know him; for he dwelleth with you, and shall be in you."[1]

When the Lord indwells us with his Spirit, he does great things for us through the Scripture. "Holy men of God spake as they were moved by the Holy Ghost."[2] Therefore, when we come to the Scriptures, we find that the Holy Spirit is the Author of Scripture.

"Eye hath not seen, nor ear heard, neither have entered into the heart of man, the things which God hath prepared for them that love him. But God has revealed them unto us by his Spirit."[3] So the Holy Spirit is also the Revealer of Scripture.

Settle it as one of the simplest resolutions, to make time every day to read God's Word. Study it quietly, unhurriedly, believingly, prayerfully and obediently, that Christ may be revealed by the Spirit in the Scriptures to you.

The Holy Spirit and the New Christian

Becoming a Christian is not a matter of turning over a new leaf; it is a matter of receiving a new life. How? It is by the Holy Spirit.

The Holy Spirit does a difficult and a challenging and a cutting work. He convicts of sin. We read in John 16 that the Holy Spirit, when he comes, convinces the world of sin, because they believe not on Jesus.[4]

But of course the Holy Spirit loves to conspire together with our Savior the Lord Jesus, not only in convicting of sin, but in cleansing from sin: "The blood of Jesus Christ . . . cleanseth us from all sin."[5]

The Lord Jesus by his Spirit gives a wholly new life: "He that believeth on the Son hath everlasting life."[6] Not just a human life, but a divine life. The law of biogenesis says that there is no life without antecedent life, and that the life we receive is the same sort of life as the one who gives it to us.

Therefore the life that is given by the Holy Spirit of God to those who believe on Jesus is the life of God; and that is why it is everlasting life.

The Holy Spirit and Growth in Grace

How does the Holy Spirit help us to grow in grace?

• By the Scriptures. We feed our souls by the Spirit of our blessed Lord and through the Scriptures. When I was ordained, I wondered, as I was committed to proclaim the Word for the rest of my days, if it might become threadbare to me. Thank God it has not become threadbare; I am just beginning to scratch the surface of the Book. I find new and unplumbed depths in God's Word. We will grow in grace as we keep close to God's Word and the Spirit opens our eyes to its truths.

• By the gift of prayer. Don't think of prayer in terms of getting things from God; think of prayer as the natural breath of the Christian. I love the work of the Spirit in prayer: "The Spirit also helpeth our infirmities: for we know not what we should pray for as we ought: but the Spirit itself maketh intercession for us with groanings which cannot be uttered. And he that searcheth the hearts knoweth what is the mind of the Spirit, because he maketh intercession for the saints according to the will of God."[7]

Don't think that prayer has to be complicated. It isn't. Anything that concerns us concerns God. Any people we try to reach and to touch interest him. We need to bring to God not just ourselves and our interests, but all the interests of the world and the mission field.

• By abiding in Christ. The gracious Holy Spirit prompts us to live close to Jesus; and Jesus says to us, "Abide in me."[8] To abide in Christ is, first, to have no conscious shadow of sin between ourselves and Jesus; and, second, consciously to draw all our grace and strength from Christ by his Spirit in our daily living.

• By the surrender of your will to Jesus Christ. We read in Romans 12:1: "I beseech you therefore, brethren, by the mercies of God, that ye present your bodies a living sacrifice, holy, acceptable unto God, which is your reasonable service."[9] In Ephesians 4:30 we read, "Grieve not the holy Spirit of God."[10]

Do not grieve the Spirit of our God, who comes in great power in the symbol of the wind which sweeps along to do the will of

God. Surrender to his will.

• By the infilling of the Spirit. In Ephesians 5:18 we read, "Be filled with the Spirit."[11] This does not mean that we have to agonize and try to have more of the power of Christ's Spirit, but that we have so to yield ourselves to Jesus Christ as Lord, that the Person of Christ's Spirit has all of us. Then we may rejoice in the cleansing and the conquering and the keeping power of the Spirit of our risen Lord Jesus in our hearts and lives.

The Holy Spirit and Equipment for Christian Service

Each one of us has some gift given by the Spirit to be consecrated back to God for love of Jesus and for service of mankind: "He gave some, apostles; and some, prophets; and some, evangelists; and some, pastors and teachers; For the perfecting of the saints, for the work of the ministry, for the edifying of the body of Christ."[12]

If we know Jesus as our Savior, and if the Holy Spirit has given us new life in Christ, we can be sure that he may have a new work for us. Ask for a task suited to the gifts that the Spirit of God has given to you. Seek his will for your service. He calls, he equips and he sanctifies that we may serve him.

If you are an older Christian, you may be wondering whether the work of God is narrowing for you. But as the years go by, though physically you may not have the same stamina and strength as of old, the work of God doesn't narrow. It only goes deeper.

The Holy Spirit of God wants to touch our hearts and make Jesus real to us. He wants to build us up in the faith of Christ and make us strong, stable, mature Christians. He wants to equip us for the great privilege of Christian service; and this he loves to do. It isn't our ability; it's our yieldedness to him. It isn't our strength; it is Christ's Spirit dwelling in the surrendered heart that can bring new light to others.

---

(1) John 14:16-17, KJV. (2) 2 Peter 1:21, KJV. (3) 1 Corinthians 2:9-10, KJV. (4) John 16:8-9. (5) 1 John 1:7, KJV. (6) John 3:36, KJV. (7) Romans 8:26-27, KJV. (8) John 15:4, KJV. (9) Romans 12:1, KJV. (10) Ephesians 4:30, KJV. (11) Ephesians 5:18, KJV. (12) Ephesians 4:11-12, KJV

Quiet Nudges

Lorraine Joy Burt

My heart sank and my foot on the gas pedal felt weak as I was speeding over the hill. Just ahead a police car was parked on the side of the street. I slowed down, hoping the patrolman wouldn't notice me. It didn't work. I heard the siren behind me.

I was disgusted with myself and embarrassed as people drove by and stared. The officer seemed to take "forever" writing out the speeding ticket.

That evening, as I reviewed the day's activities, I had a feeling of dissatisfaction with myself. It was as if my heart were crying, "Why, Lord, did it have to happen? You know I've got a lot to do and I can't be bothered with anything extra." It was at that point that the Lord spoke to me.

Earlier I had come across an article by Philip Yancey, who had written about the "quiet nudges God [uses] to guide us without overwhelming us." Hadn't a friend commented the preceding day

Lorraine Joy Burt is a free-lance writer and a substitute teacher. She and her husband, James, are the parents of two children. They live in Woodbury, Minnesota, where they attend Woodbury United Methodist Church. ©1988 Billy Graham Evangelistic Association.

on my driving too fast? That was a quiet nudge from the Holy Spirit. Yet I excused myself, saying I had to accelerate to get up the approach ramp.

When I mentioned the "quiet nudges" in Sunday school class where we were looking at ways the Holy Spirit works in our lives, the pastor responded, "Quiet nudges sound great, but how many of us are living in such a way that we feel the nudges?"

My friend's gentle reprimand should have been adequate to warn me about following the posted limits, but, as the pastor had said, I didn't feel the nudge. So the next day, instead of a quiet nudge, the Lord had allowed a screaming siren on a squad car. It was as if the Lord were saying to me, "Yes, I'm willing to use quiet nudges to help you to 'walk by the Spirit,' or in this case, to drive with the Spirit's self-control, but you weren't listening. The only way to get your attention was with the siren screaming in your ear."

"Yes, Lord, I get the message. I'm sorry that I lacked self-control. Thank You for making this indiscretion painful for me so that I will be more careful the next time I am behind the wheel."

I have determined that throughout each day I will be alert to the Holy Spirit's working in my life. For example, one Sunday afternoon when I was about to sit down and relax with the newspaper, I suddenly remembered a relative whom I knew was lonely. I silently thanked the Lord for the quiet nudge and proceeded to follow through by visiting with my relative for part of the afternoon. Familiar Scripture came to my mind: "Inasmuch as ye have done it unto one of the least of these my brethren, ye have done it unto me."[1]

I have come to realize that there is an effort required of us if we are to progress in the Christian life. But we need to trust God and rest in him so that we can be aware of his quiet nudges.

The author of the following prayer was apparently learning to be patient too: "Slow me down, Lord. Remind me each day of the fable of the hare and the tortoise, that I may know that the race is not always to the swift, that there is more to life than increasing its speed. Let me look upward into the branches of the towering oak and know that it grew great and strong because it grew slowly and well."[2]

---

(1) Matthew 25:40, KJV. (2) Quoted in "Fruit of the Spirit," by Stephen F. Winward, ©1981 Stephen F. Winward, Inter-Varsity Press, Leicester, England, Wm. B. Eerdmans Publishing Company, Grand Rapids, Michigan

"You Are!"

Kathy Guinn

I still didn't have an answer to my question of many years: Why did God call himself "I AM"? Somehow the name just didn't make much sense to me.

Moses asked God, "When I come unto the children of Israel, and shall say unto them, The God of your fathers hath sent me unto you; and they shall say to me, What is his name? what shall I say unto them? And God said unto Moses, I AM THAT I AM: and he said, Thus shalt thou say unto the children of Israel, I AM hath sent me unto you" (Exodus 3:13-14, KJV).

Why didn't God just say, "I am God almighty" or, "I am Jehovah" or, "I am eternal" or . . . Why did he say just "I AM"? It sounded so incomplete, but then who am I to question God? I concluded it would be another unanswered question that would have to wait until Eternity.

Thinking that the subject was closed, I put my Bible aside and dropped to my knees for my prayer time. "Dear beloved Father, I am overwhelmed as I realize Your greatness. After all, You are

Kathy Guinn is a free-lance writer and a kindergarten teacher's aide. She and her husband, Noah, are the parents of four children (one deceased). They make their home in Okemah, Oklahoma. ©1985 Kathy Guinn.

Eternal. You are True, Faithful, Light, Love, Almighty, Comfort. God, You are . . ."

And then I couldn't think of any more descriptions. Words had failed me, but I wanted to try and express what I felt. Haltingly, I continued: "Father, You are . . . You are . . . You are!"

What peace came as I realized that simple phrase was the grand total! "God, You Are!" I cried with new appreciation, as I understood to a small degree God saying, "I AM."

◆ ◆ ◆

Almighty God,
   I am secure
   knowing You are firmly
   in control of my universe.
Small, distressing events,
   thorn-in-the-flesh circumstances,
   and sometimes shattering calamities
   continually threaten my world.
Knowing You are undebatably Master,
   non-negotiably sovereign,
   is more than reassuring;
   it is vital.
I can weather the storm,
   cupped within Your hands;
   I know that Your love
   will soon calm the angry waves.
   —PATRICIA JARACZ
     Riverdale, Illinois

2

Forgiveness From God Today

"As far as the east is from the west, so far has he removed our transgressions from us."
Psalm 103:12, NIV

Dig Out the Root of Bitterness

James Hilt

Anger may come and go, but bitter feelings often remain for years. In counseling I have met many people, including the elderly, whose bitterness began in their youth. This is why the writer of Hebrews aptly called it a "bitter root."[1] For, like a root, bitterness can grow and spread for years, entangling our attitudes, feelings and thoughts.

Why do people become bitter? First, every person has a strong need to love and be unconditionally loved, to feel worthwhile to himself and to others. Each of us is equipped with a mental radar which detects whether or not these needs are being met.

If a person registers a negative message, he feels cheated or robbed of something he intuitively knows should be his. Seeds of anger may then germinate which, if nourished by further evidences of unmet needs, grow into a root of bitterness.

Don, a young man in his teens, longed for love from his parents—love without any strings attached. Coupled with this was a deep

James Hilt is director of counseling for Chapel of the Air in Wheaton, Illinois, and co-author of the book "How to Dispose of Negative Feelings." He and his wife, Karen, are the parents of one son and live in West Chicago. They attend Bloomingdale Community Church. ©1983 James Hilt.

hunger for their approval, especially his father's. Yet these deep longings remained unsatisfied.

Though his father was a committed Christian and a pastor, Don was bombarded with such nonverbal messages as: "If you get good grades, excel in sports and prove to be a good Christian model, then I will love and accept you."

Thus, in Don's mind his acceptability in his father's eyes depended on certain performance levels reached. Because everything had to be earned, everything was conditional. Consequently, always having to prove himself, Don felt cheated and deeply wounded inside, with a festering bitterness toward his father.

All too often I come across people who, like Don, were emotionally abused by conditional love and acceptance from parents and others. They are torn apart inside by a love that is not secure, not a gift, and therefore unlike the love of Christ. They need to learn that God's love is like sunlight: one can do nothing to either lessen or intensify its power, but only bask in its warmth.[2]

A second reason for bitterness is personal loss. Losing something or someone may seem to be intolerable, impossible to accept. Mental revolt occurs which causes, then feeds, the bitterness.

Because we live in a hazardous, fallen world, many kinds of losses are possible. Financial loss is an example. An overwhelming wave of bitterness came in the wake of the great crash of 1929. Unable to accept and endure a sudden reversal of fortune, many people bitterly reacted by ending their lives. Other painful losses include loss of health, a job, meaning in life, self-respect or a spouse through divorce or death.

Several losses occurring together are especially apt to provoke bitterness. Consider Job. Having lost his dear children, livestock and health, he cried out: "I loathe my very life; therefore I will give free rein to my complaint and speak out in the bitterness of my soul."[3]

Sinful attitudes can also cause bitterness. God so created human nature that when sinful attitudes such as envy, jealousy and pride emerge, a person can be drawn down a path leading to bitterness.

It is evident that jealousy and pride triggered King Saul's bitterness. Following David's conquest of Goliath, women in a festive mood played musical instruments and sang songs praising David.[4]

Saul immediately burned with jealousy and wounded pride, both of which triggered bitterness. He found it intolerable that a young, unknown sheepherder could detract from his "glorious popularity" among the people.

Bitterness acts like acid or cancer. It eats away at our emotional, physical and spiritual health. Bitterness destroys relationships. This is because, when infected with bitterness, the mind instinctively draws upon its resources to plan and initiate acts of vengeance. This process is like a nation mobilizing its human and natural assets to wage war successfully. This explains why so many actions and words have "attack" overtones.

Think again of Saul. Embittered, he was consumed by the drive for revenge. For years he ruthlessly stalked David, only to end up going insane and being killed in battle. Bitterness sets into motion powerful forces of destruction, both in our minds and in our relationships.

Are you bitter? If so, you need to dig out that bitter root, to heed Paul's words: "Get rid of all bitterness."[5]

Here are four steps which can bring needed healing. First, confess the bitterness as sin to Christ. Perhaps you have suffered a great loss or have been deeply wounded by another. Nevertheless, do not try to justify your reaction or explain it away. A bitter reaction needs to be confessed, regardless of the cause. Having confessed, be sure to breathe in God's full, unconditional forgiveness.[6]

Second, ask God for the power to accept fully the source of bitterness. Ask him to help you remove the mental revolt connected with it. Often our minds fixate on what has hurt or offended us. Its memory is replayed incessantly. But this only narrows the field of consciousness, driving away positive, wholesome thoughts. So instead of mentally replaying the offense like a record, take the needle off.

Does this sound difficult or even impossible? Sometimes we are truly powerless to accept certain blows or setbacks in life. This is why only God is able to grant the power to accept them, and the only way for us to receive this power is to ask him for it.

Acceptance, however, does not mean that we must somehow relish our hurt or count it as good. Many afflictions result from evil forces in the world and should never be seen as less than evil! Acceptance is not the same as approval.

God detests and is angered by all evil. We must detest it too. Christ can be thanked, however, for how he can work even through evil to bring about good into our lives.[7] There is a big difference between praising God for evil and thanking him for faithfully bearing fruit through it.

Third, ask Christ for the power to forgive every offender, those whose actions precipitated the bitterness. Notice in Ephesians 4:31-32 that Paul commands us to "get rid of all bitterness," and then immediately to "be kind and compassionate to one another, forgiving each other, just as in Christ God forgave you."[8]

"But the person who hurt me doesn't deserve to be forgiven," you may say. Forgive him in your mind anyway. If he has truly wronged you and not yet repented, he still bears his guilt. He is still accountable to God.

Forgiveness releases the pressure of steam which can otherwise build up, causing great mental stress. It is a wonderful therapeutic device which cleanses, heals and brings increased love, peace and strength to the mind. Forgiveness is not a grudging burden, but an experience of relief and joy! Forgive each one by name. If self-directed bitterness exists, forgive yourself as well.

Fourth, ask Christ to heal you of all the bitterness you hold toward others, God and yourself. Allow him to dig up what perhaps has been growing like a root for years.

---

(1) Hebrews 12:15, NIV. (2) Psalm 36:5-10; Romans 15:7; 1 John 4. (3) Job 10:1, NIV. (4) 1 Samuel 18:7. (5) Ephesians 4:31, NIV. (6) 1 John 1:9. (7) Romans 8:28. (8) Ephesians 4:31-32, NIV. Bible verses marked NIV are taken by permission from The Holy Bible, New International Version, copyright ©1973, 1978, 1984 International Bible Society, East Brunswick, New Jersey

"I'm Learning How to Forgive"

David V. Kiel, as told to Ann Lunde

Nobody's gonna rip me off!" the angry customer shouted. "I just paid you!"

As he ranted and raved, vile words poured from his mouth. I remained composed and unaffected.

Suddenly he stormed off. "He's going to get the $13," I thought as I waited in the living room. "I'll have a perfect collection record!"

The welcomed silence lasted only a few moments. Suddenly there was a deafening explosion. When I awoke, I was on the floor. I couldn't move. Blood was streaming out of my mouth. Something was dreadfully wrong!

Twice I blacked out. When I finally awoke, I was in a hospital in a canvas strap apparatus called a Stryker Frame. From the nurses I pieced together what had happened. I had been shot in the back with a .38-calibre revolver. The bullet had hit just below the seventh cervical vertebra. Emergency measures used by the paramedics had probably saved my life. The injury to the spinal cord, however,

David V. Kiel received a degree in technical illustration and is a free-lance architectural illustrator working as a sub-contractor to graphics departments of local businesses. Ann Lunde is a homemaker and a free-lance writer. She and her husband, Stuart, are the parents of three children and live in Hilo, Hawaii. ©1985 Ann Lunde.

had caused permanent paralysis from the upper chest downward. Doctors said I would never walk again. It was January 20, 1977.

Someone had told our church prayer chain of the emergency. Christians were praying, comforting my wife and looking after our two small children. Church elders were sitting outside my hospital room praying. Even the surgeon had prayed before removing the bullet.

I remained critically ill for weeks. Finally my condition stabilized and I was transferred to our state rehabilitation center. The atmosphere of the center and Scripture studies on my own encouraged me. I came home with a positive attitude. However, in the following months and years, my positive attitude slowly eroded.

I found my mind concentrating on the incident. Why had it happened to me, a Christian? What about the man who did it? Here I was unable to care for many of my own personal needs, and he was still walking around out there on two good legs and feet. The more I rehashed these thoughts, the worse my attitude became. Struggling with intense pain, I became nervous and irritable. I was overcome with self-pity.

A Christian friend saw what was happening and confronted me. "The Lord wants you to know that your attitude stinks!" he said bluntly.

"How do you know what the Lord thinks?" I retorted. But inwardly I knew he was right. Bitterness was poisoning my soul. It was separating me from God. I would have to forgive the man who shot me. But I couldn't do it. I really didn't want to.

I prayed many times in the weeks and months that followed. I forced myself to pray for that man. As I did, a degree of compassion for him grew within me. Though I was severely handicapped, I had Jesus to lean upon. The man who shot me probably did not. My attitude began to improve.

Life around me was crumbling, however. Centered on my own troubles, I had failed to recognize the warning signals. My wife withdrew from Christian activities and Christian friends. She became bored with attending church. She seldom opened her Bible. She was restless and talked of being "unfulfilled" as a woman. She left for a week to think things through; when she returned, she explained that she could no longer handle being the wife of a quadriplegic. She wanted a divorce.

Within three days she was gone. Our children, their pictures, my tools, the china and most of the furniture went with her. I was alone in an empty house.

Many nights I maneuvered my wheelchair in circles in the middle of the living room. I turned on all the lights, the radio, the television, just to make it seem as if someone were with me. The Scriptures I shouted to the walls echoed back at me.

But as I turned to God's Word, Scripture took on new significance. I began to study God's promises daily, and day after day I tried to depend on those promises.

Still, adjustment was not easy. My beloved children were being raised in a non-Christian atmosphere. In the divorce she won custody of the children, received half interest in the house, plus child support and social security for the children. Then, she found someone to marry and became financially well off. Everything she did seemed to prosper while I struggled financially. Unable to find a job, my only support was the money I received from the state.

After visiting the kids, I would arrive home, overcome with "whys" and "how-comes." Though I seemed to be growing spiritually, depression, self-pity and bitterness were still problems in my life. Again it was a Christian friend who confronted me. And again I didn't like what he said. But I had to admit that God had spoken through him. Yes, I was carrying resentment. Yes, it was affecting my relationship with God. And yes, I had to do something about it. "I surrender this bitterness to You, Lord," I prayed. "Give me Your attitude toward my ex-wife and toward my handicap."

Forgiveness was a real struggle for me. I couldn't seem to do it on my own. I had to depend on the Lord Jesus Christ to change my heart. And he did this through time and his Word.

I repeated and memorized pertinent Scriptures. As I did this, I began to see things from God's point of view. My family needed the Lord. Who was interceding for them? Recognizing that I was still the spiritual head of my family, I began praying daily that my ex-wife would return to Jesus. I entrusted my children daily to his care. I asked God to connect them with God-fearing people and to protect them from negative peer pressure. My struggles with my attitude became easier. The circumstances were the same, but I was improving.

I needed to get out of myself. I began investing time and love in other people's lives. As I did so, God slowly healed the hurts inside me. Somehow, today they're not as painful as they were. I have grown used to a situation I cannot change. I have shifted my attention from what was done to me, to what I can do for Jesus.

It's surprising how a person's viewpoint changes when things
are right inside. Through my affliction I have learned patience—
patience with other people and with myself. For me, learning to
forgive has been a long, lengthy process. I know today, however,
that bitterness is something I simply cannot afford to have in my
life. I want to make every moment count for Jesus Christ.

◆ ◆ ◆

If I could
    I would
drag you kicking,
to his feet,
put your hand in his,
    stand back
and watch your hardness
melt away,
excuses disappear,
as you see him
    face to face
but this I cannot do
(nor he).
I cannot break
the walls you build
nor change your heart
if you would not
so I will be a friend to you
and show you love
    and share his fruits
that in some quiet moment
you will know
that he is real,
that you have seen him
    face to face.
        —ANNE W. MURPHY
        Shermansdale, Pennsylvania

Forgiveness:
A New Beginning

Billy Graham

Psychologists, sociologists and psychiatrists all recognize that there is something wrong with man. Many words in Scripture describe it. Among them is the word "transgression": "Sin is the transgression of the law."[1] What law? The Law of Moses, the Ten Commandments. Have you ever broken one of those Commandments? Then you are guilty of having broken all of them. A second word, "sin," carries with it the idea of missing the mark, coming short of our duty, failure to do what we ought to do. The Bible says, "All unrighteousness is sin."[2] And yet before we can get to heaven, we must have righteousness. God says, "Be perfect as I am perfect, holy as I am holy."[3] Where are we going to get that perfection? We don't have it now. Yet we can't get to heaven if we don't have it. That is why Christ died on the cross; he shed his blood and rose again to provide righteousness for us.

A third word is "iniquity," which is turning aside from the straight path. Isaiah said, "All we like sheep have gone astray; we have turned every one to his own way."[4]

A man named Nicodemus came to Jesus by night. He asked Jesus some questions about spiritual life. Jesus replied, "Nicodemus, you need to be born again."[5] In fact, he said, "Verily, verily"—and any time that Jesus used that expression, he meant that what was to follow was important. He said, "Verily, verily, I say unto thee, Except a man be born again, he cannot see the kingdom of God."[6]

Have you been born again? Call it conversion, call it commitment, call it repentance, call it being saved, but has it happened to you? Does Christ live in your heart? Do you know it? Many persons have thought a long time about religion and Christianity, and yet have never made a commitment. Are you committed to Jesus Christ?

Stunned

When Jesus said to Nicodemus, "You must be born again," Nicodemus must have been stunned. He was one of the great religious leaders of his time, yet he was searching for reality. Why did Jesus say that Nicodemus must be born again? Because he could read the heart of Nicodemus. Jesus saw that Nicodemus had covered himself with religion, but had not yet found fellowship with God.

Radical

The Bible says, "Wherefore, as by one man sin entered into the world, and death by sin; and so death passed upon all men, for that all have sinned."[7] Every person needs a radical change. We need to have our sins forgiven, we need to be clothed in the righteousness of God for the purpose of finding fulfillment in this life, we need to find something to commit ourselves to. Are you a committed person? What are you committed to? Why don't you make Christ your course and follow him? He will never let you down.

Some persons ask the question: What is the new birth? Nicodemus asked that question too: "How can a man be born when he is old?"[8] Nicodemus could see only the physical and the material. Jesus was talking about the spiritual.

We cannot inherit new birth. The Bible says, "Which were born, not of blood, nor of the will of the flesh, nor of the will of man, but of God."[9] Our fathers and mothers may be the greatest born-again Christians in the world, but that doesn't make us born-again Christians too. There are many people who have the idea that because they were born into a Christian home, they are automatically Christians. But they're not.

And we cannot work our way to God. The Bible says, "Not by works of righteousness which we have done, but according to his mercy he saved us, by the washing of regeneration, and renewing of the Holy Ghost."[10]

Reformation is not enough. We can say, "I am going to turn over a new leaf, or I am going to make New Year's resolutions," but Isaiah said that in the sight of God "all our righteousnesses are as filthy rags."[11]

Changed

Some of us have changed on the outside to conform to certain social standards or behavior that is expected of us in our churches, but down inside we have never been changed. That is what Jesus was talking to Nicodemus about. He said, "Nicodemus, you need changing inside," and only the Holy Spirit can do that. Being born from above is a supernatural act of God. The Holy Spirit convicts us of our sin, disturbs us because we have sinned against God. And then the Holy Spirit regenerates us. That is when we are born again. The Holy Spirit comes to live in our hearts, to help us in our daily lives. The Spirit of God gives us assurance, gives us joy, produces fruit in our lives and teaches us the Scriptures.

Some people try to imitate Christ. They think that all we have to do is try to follow Jesus and try to do the things he did, and we will get to heaven. But we can't do it. We may know the religious-language, we may sing religious songs, we may even say prayers, but if we haven't been to the foot of the cross, we haven't been born again. That is the message Jesus is trying to teach us.

To be born again means that: "A new heart also will I give you, and a new spirit will I put within you"[12]; "Old things are passed away; behold, all things are become new"[13]; we are "partakers of the divine nature"[14]; we are "passed from death unto life."[15] The new birth brings about a change in our philosophy and manner of living.

How is it accomplished? There is a mystery to it. Jesus said, "The wind bloweth where it listeth . . . but [thou] canst not tell whence it cometh, and whither it goeth."[16] But you can see the result. Jesus did not attempt to explain the new birth to Nicodemus; our finite minds cannot understand the infinite. We come by simple childlike faith, and we put our faith in Jesus Christ. When we do, we are born again.

Incorruptible

It happens this way. First, we have to hear the Word of God: "Being born again, not of corruptible seed, but of incorruptible, by the word of God, which liveth and abideth for ever."[17] "Faith cometh by hearing, and hearing by the word of God."[18] That is the first step. "It pleased God by the foolishness of preaching"—or declaration or proclamation—"to save them that believe."[19] It sounds foolish that words out of a Bible have the power to penetrate our hearts and change our lives, but they do, because they are God's holy words.

And then there is the work of the Holy Spirit. He convicts: "And when he is come, he will reprove the world of sin, and of righteousness, and of judgment."[20] He changes us. He changes our wills, our affections, our objectives for living, our disposition. He gives us a new purpose and new goals. "Old things pass away, and everything becomes new."[21] Then he indwells us: "Know ye not that ye are the temple of God, and that the Spirit of God dwelleth in you?"[22] Does God the Holy Spirit live in you?

Jesus Christ says that we must be born again. How do we become born again? By repenting of sin. That means we are willing to change our way of living. We say to God, "I'm a sinner, and I'm sorry." It's simple and childlike. Then by faith we receive Jesus Christ as our Lord and Master and Savior. We are willing to follow him in a new life of obedience, in which the Holy Spirit helps us as we read the Bible and pray and witness.

Accepted

If there is a doubt in your mind that you have been born again, I hope you will settle it now, because the Bible says, "Now is the accepted time; . . . [today] is the day of salvation."[23]

---

(1) 1 John 3:4, KJV. (2) 1 John 5:17, KJV. (3) Cf. Matthew 5:48. (4) Isaiah 53:6, KJV. (5) Cf. John 3:3. (6) John 3:3, KJV. (7) Romans 5:12, KJV. (8) John 3:4, KJV. (9) John 1:13, KJV. (10) Titus 3:5, KJV. (11) Isaiah 64:6, KJV. (12) Ezekiel 36:22, KJV. (13) 2 Corinthians 5:17, KJV. (14) 2 Peter 1:4, KJV. (15) John 5:24, KJV. (16) John 3:8, KJV. (17) 1 Peter 1:23, KJV. (18) Romans 10:17, KJV. (19) 1 Corinthians 1:21, KJV. (20) John 16:8, KJV. (21) Cf. 2 Corinthians 5:17. (22) 1 Corinthians 3:16, KJV. (23) 2 Corinthians 6:2, KJV

"A Mark on My Heart"

Jane Frank

I stepped out of the doctor's office with news that would have brought joy to most women. But for me it was a verdict of guilt. I was pregnant.

Mechanically, I guided my little car to Jerry's house. "Let's go for a ride," I said, trying to talk over the television set. Maybe it was the note of hysteria in my voice, or maybe just that I spoke unusually loudly, but Jerry leaped to his feet. We drove the few blocks to our "dreaming spot," the place where we first talked about love, where we had said that we would get married some day.

"Jer, the test is positive," I said. I lifted my eyes to catch his response, but he wouldn't look at me. Fear gripped my heart. I was afraid he would leave me to face this on my own. Soon I was sobbing.

Jerry pulled me to him. "I'm sorry," he said and held me tightly. "Don't worry, honey, things will work out. What did the doctor say?"

Jane Frank is a homemaker and co-founder of Conquerors (a post-abortion support group) and author of the pamphlet "What They Won't Tell You at the Abortion Clinic." She and her husband, Jerry, are the parents of three children and live in Crystal, Minnesota. They attend a Christian and Missionary Alliance church. ©1985 Jane Frank.

"The doctor didn't doubt that some day I would make a good mother," I said, "but not now, not at 18. He suggested that I check into having an abortion." We sat in silence for a while, both of us staring off through the windows.

"Our parents would kill us if they knew you were pregnant!" Jerry finally broke the silence. Jerry's mom and dad were charter members of their church, well known and well respected in the community. My parents were convinced that Jerry and I were a "nice Christian couple." Any sort of testimony I had would be destroyed if I had a baby out of wedlock.

We wanted to be married—that had already been planned, but where would Jerry get a job to support me and our baby? Would our love for each other be able to withstand the pressure of an unwelcome child in another six months? Would we be able to bear the gossip and finger-pointing? Every question brought the easy answer to my mind: "Just have an abortion and you can go on with your life."

The next day I went to work in a fog. After I made the same clerical error three times, my friend, Joyce, sensed that something was wrong and suggested we take our lunch break together. Before long the whole story came spilling out.

"I don't know what to do," I whispered, as tears started.

"Well," she began, "a few years ago I was in a situation like you. I had an abortion because I really thought Mike would dump me if I didn't. If you want to have it done, I know of a place. I could give you the phone number this afternoon."

Later that day I dialed the number Joyce had given me. In a few minutes I had an appointment to see a counselor the following Tuesday.

Tuesday afternoon I followed a counselor down a sterile white corridor and into a small examining room. After my examination she led me to a counseling room. "We get girls like you in every day," she stated. "You're young, unmarried, and you have no means to support yourself and a baby. You are 12 weeks along, and I would suggest that you have the procedure done soon, preferably by the end of the week. It takes a short time and the recovery period is usually half an hour."

With that, my "counseling session" was over. I felt more hopeless and confused than before. The counselor had never mentioned having the baby and working things out or giving it up for adoption. They scheduled me for an abortion that Friday afternoon.

I knew that abortion was wrong, but I couldn't put a finger on why I felt that way. I looked for someone to talk me out of it. I asked co-workers if they would ever consider abortion as a solution to an unwanted pregnancy, but I got no solid answers. I called a pastor and told him that my friend was pregnant. "What should I tell her?" I asked. "She's not married and wants to have an abortion." Inside I was begging him to tell me abortion was wrong. "Show me something from Scripture," I silently pleaded.

"I guess in some circumstances it might be right, but personally I don't believe . . ." He dashed my hopes of finding a concrete reason why my spirit was against abortion.

Friday came and my heart was still unconvinced that I was doing right. A woman at the clinic shoved some papers at me to sign.

Numb, I waited in my assigned room while a doctor and an assistant set up their equipment. Soon I heard the roar of the vacuum aspiration machine.

"Have you had morning sickness?" the nurse asked. "Oh, you'll feel great tonight! No more queasiness. Tomorrow you'll be 100 percent again."

During the first few days after my abortion, relief far outweighed the guilt I felt. Now I could go back to being the "nice Christian girl" without anyone being the wiser. I immersed myself in wedding plans. Jerry and I were married, and the wedding was flawless.

But afterward I felt let down. I had a hole in my heart.

For the next eight years I sought to fill the void in my life. I tried to be a good wife and mother, but I felt tainted. Yet I didn't connect my severed relationship with God to my abortion.

Shortly after our third child was born, I went to work at an insurance company. While some co-workers and I sat stuffing envelopes, our friend Kay told us about her recent absence from work; she had had a miscarriage at 12 weeks.

"This miscarriage was one of several I have had, but it was different," she said. "This one was harder to handle because I went into labor and gave birth to a perfectly formed, two-and-a-half-inch child. I could count all the little fingers and toes; it was incredible!"

The full impact of what Kay said washed over me like a suffocating wave. My abortion had not removed a growth, a blob of tissue, as I had been told; it had destroyed a baby. Before this, I had assumed that I had merely removed some unwanted tissue that had the potential of becoming a child. What I had gotten rid of was a baby. I was guilty of murder.

Seeing the truth about abortion hurt deeply, but it set me on the road to spiritual and emotional healing. For months I battled depression, anger and shame. I constantly thought about my baby, pondering how things could have been different.

Through a local crisis pregnancy center, I got in touch with a support group to help women deal with their abortion experiences. The counselor's warmth and enthusiasm made me feel as if I were talking with an old friend. She told me that it was OK, healthy in fact, to grieve for my baby. It was the repression of that grief for so many years that had wrought emotional problems.

In the next weeks Kathy showed me how to get rid of the remorse I felt by believing God's Word that I was forgiven in Christ Jesus. I had often based my relationship with God on the shaky ground of my feelings. But I learned that God's love doesn't waver. Romans 8:33-39, which talks about God's love, became my verses for survival.

As I allowed the natural grieving cycle to complete itself, I saw that it was up to me either to wallow in the past and let my failures engulf me, or to allow God to use me for his work.

Now Jerry and I are warning others of the trauma an abortion can cause. When a woman is pregnant, she *knows* that there is a baby in her body, a real life. She will have some feeling about that child, no matter what happens to him. Abortion is not the easy solution that people say it is. I know that it is hard to have a baby and raise it alone or to give it up for adoption, but I would rather know in my heart that I let my child live than to say, "My baby was an inconvenience to me, so I killed it."

Even though I know that there is forgiveness in Christ, my lost baby has left a mark on my heart.

3

Seeking God's Character Today

"Be imitators of God . . . and live a life of love, just as Christ loved us and gave himself up for us."
Ephesians 5:1-2, NIV

Learning the Meaning of Mercy

Glenyce Coffin

The blackboard in my third grade classroom had a list of the names of several of my pupils. After their names were checks, indicating their misdemeanors.

Glancing at the students and at the blackboard, I had a pang of guilt. I thought, "My name should be there too, for being irritable all day."

I paused with that dark thought, then suddenly I brightened. I knew it was time to explain to my students the meaning of the word "mercy."

They perked up when I moved to the blackboard and began to talk softly about the names listed there. I reminded them that each knew why his or her name was on the board and the reason for each check. They nodded silently, knowing the system.

"But," I continued, reaching for the eraser, "I'll have mercy on you. Does anyone know what that word means?" Nobody did.

Silently, dramatically, I erased all the names and all the check

Glenyce Coffin is an elementary school teacher at Ponemah Elementary School in Ponemah, Minnesota. She and her husband, Russel, are the parents of four children and live in Puposky. The Coffins attend First Presbyterian Church in Bemidji. ©1986 Billy Graham Evangelistic Association.

marks. A sigh of relief spread throughout the room, and the tension that had built up steadily during the day evaporated.

"That's mercy," I said. "You broke our class rules and deserved punishment, but I forgive you and I'm setting you free." I said that I would carry no grudges into the next day and that they were free to begin with a clean slate.

God shows us much greater mercy when he forgives us. As sinners we deserve punishment, but he offers to erase our sins. His mercies are grandly "new every morning."[1]

Mercy—The Character of God

God doesn't only *show* mercy to us; he *is* merciful. Mercy is an integral part of his character and he is bound to exhibit it.

Many of the Old Testament leaders depended on that fact to initiate turnabouts in their lives as well as to lead their people in his ways. Daniel prayed, "We do not present our supplications before thee on the ground of our righteousness, but on the ground of thy great mercy."[2] His prayer was typical of those prayed by Moses, Jacob, Solomon, Nehemiah and Jonah when they wanted results from God.

David was once given a choice of three punishments by the prophet Gad. David didn't take long to decide: "Let us fall into the hand of the Lord, for his mercy is great; but let me not fall into the hand of man."[3] He could not depend on man to wield judgment without undue harshness or vindication. From God he expected judgment, but fair judgment, tempered with mercy. And that is exactly what he received.

Mercy—Balanced With Justice

It didn't take long for one of my third graders to conclude that he had stumbled on to a good thing. His teacher wasn't interested only in justice, she also cared about mercy. Every time his name went on the board, he appealed for mercy with a smart-alecky touch, as if he had discovered a soft spot in his teacher's character.

That's often the trouble we run into when we practice mercy. The Israelites attempted to stretch God's mercy to the limit until he became angry with them. Though God forgave them repeatedly, he wanted to teach them his obligation to justice too. In his book about Ezekiel, Stuart Briscoe describes this balance of mercy and justice: "The mercy of God was still tugging at the coattails of his justice."[4]

Justice alone can be harsh and cold. Mercy alone can seem spineless. One must temper justice with mercy. This means that decisions about individuals are made not only in terms of acts and consequences but also with loving concern for them.

God listened to Moses' intercession for his rebellious people and *chose* to honor Moses' intercession. In doing this, he chose to act from the mercy side of his character instead of from the justice side. But God remains in control, no matter which facet of his character he exhibits.

Isaiah tells us, "Therefore the Lord waits to be gracious to you; therefore he exalts himself to show mercy to you. For the Lord is a God of justice; blessed are all those who wait for him."[5]

Imagine how grateful Jonah was that "the mercy of God was . . . tugging at the coattails of his justice" long ago. And, knowing our own failures, how grateful we are today!

Mercy—A Powerful Prayer

Many times, in the middle of busy days, a prayer for mercy runs through my mind, deep underneath conscious thoughts. When circumstances aren't going well and I'm in an emotional turmoil, I hear myself silently repeating that plea for mercy. It gives my unsteady emotions a bedrock of stability, perhaps because throwing myself on God's mercy reminds me that he never changes, regardless of what is going on around or inside me.

The Canaanite woman found great power in her prayer for mercy.[6] She knew of the mercy of Jesus and this knowledge gave her great faith. That faith moved Jesus to heal her child.

The tax collector who prayed in the Temple with the Pharisee also received an answer to his prayer for mercy. He went on his way a cleansed man.[7]

I wonder if that simple prayer, "Have mercy on me," is effective because it automatically acknowledges our own helplessness. When we can't find solutions to our problems, we are driven by our needs to ask humbly for his mercy.

I was not moved to grant mercy to that smart-aleck student in my classroom; nor is God, when we seek his mercy with pride or unrepentant attitudes. But honest humility taps God's mercy.

One time, when I felt the symptoms of a cold coming on, the only prayer for healing I said was, "Lord, have mercy on me." As that prayer echoed within me over a period of several hours, my cold dried up. Like people healed in Jesus' day, I experienced the power from a simple prayer.

Mercy—Extending It to Others

David, perhaps like no other, extolled God's mercy. It had been demonstrated to him many times. But he didn't hoard God's mercies to himself—he extended them to others. A graphic example of this was when David, after being pursued mercilessly by Saul, found him asleep and vulnerable, yet chose not to kill him.[8]

Jesus taught, "Blessed are the merciful, for they shall obtain mercy."[9] It's a cycle: we receive mercy, we extend it to others, we then receive it back from others. We can extend mercy to others because God dwells in us and gives us that quality of his nature. We are merciful because we have his Spirit.

A few years ago, when I taught sixth graders, one of my students illustrated this ability to extend mercy.

Nat, a boy large for his age, loved to draw and was deeply satisfied during art class. One day, however, a smaller boy kept needling him. Nat continued to concentrate on his art project, refusing to rise to the baiting remarks.

Finally Nat reached his limit. Lifting his head, he calmly looked his classmate in the eyes and said softly, "I *could* cream you, but I *choose* to have mercy on you." The heckler quickly withdrew and Nat quietly went on with his work. He probably didn't know the Scripture verse: "It is of the Lord's mercies that we are not consumed, because his compassions fail not."[10] But his teacher did, and I'll always think of Nat when I deliberately choose to demonstrate God's mercies to others or when I feel his great mercy reaching me.

---

(1) Lamentations 3:23, RSV. (2) Daniel 9:18, RSV. (3) 2 Samuel 24:14, RSV. (4) From "All Things Weird and Wonderful," by Stuart Briscoe, ©1977 SP Publications, Inc., Victor Books, Wheaton, Illinois. (5) Isaiah 30:18, RSV. (6) Matthew 15:22-28. (7) Luke 18:10-14. (8) 1 Samuel 26. (9) Matthew 5:7, KJV. (10) Lamentations 3:22, KJV

Compassion

Roger C. Palms

T hat our world faces a dreaded illness in AIDS, no one doubts. Suddenly, in the course of only a few years, we are being hit from all sides with news releases, frightening statistics and the agony of persons who know they have this affliction and are facing death.

Much is said or thought, "It could have been avoided," or, "This doesn't concern me."

But people concern us all, and people in desperate need of hope need us most. While some AIDS victims are only angry, others are saying, "I'm sorry." They are saying it to their families and to God. But, even when a person is absolutely certain that he has given himself by confession and faith to the saving Lord Jesus Christ and is given the biblical assurance of heaven, he still has AIDS! So do those who are the innocents—who are ill and suffering through no act of their own.

Compassion is needed. Not patronizing words or smug reminders of sin, but compassion that is deep and brings a heart response that is real. That doesn't mean a winking at transgression or a denial of wrong. Nor does it mean overlooking the attitude of those rebellious ones who seem determined to use their remaining strength to curse God for not having taken AIDS out of the world, so it wouldn't be here for them to get. There is no reasoning with emotional anger. But more AIDS victims are dismayed, overwhelmed, hurt. They aren't rebelling, they are wondering.

To them, at least, we owe the care of Jesus. Maybe the love of God shown by us will spread too. It will, if those who have learned the forgiveness of Jesus will tell another about it. And if another tells another, then even the most angry or rebellious will have to listen as, dying person to dying person, they hear what is told about Christ.

Don't hold back on love. If only one suffering person comes to genuine repentance and faith and discovers the meaning of new life because you helped, he will know another whom you do not know and that person will know another. Where, then, will your compassion end? What limits are there to Christian love?

Your majesty envelopes the heavens.
    Your creativity blesses us
With the peacefulness of the rainbow.
    Your gentle hand is over us.
You're guiding our footsteps
    And comforting us when we fall.
  Through the serenity of mountain streams,
    You whisper Your love.
By the towering mountains,
    You encourage us to be strong.
As the fair meadow renews in its loveliness,
    So we renew our faith in You—
        Our Creator, Redeemer.
    —LORI AUSTIN
    Spokane, Washington

The Beauty of Lowliness

Daniel E. Fountain

L owliness and liberty are mother and child. Being poor in spirit is the prerequisite of being free. Christ, our example, became poor for us that we might become rich in the spiritual realm. He calls us to be poor for the sake of others that they also might find the true riches.

What a difficult lesson this is: to be lowly, to become poor. Yet it is the most rewarding, the most liberating, lesson in Christ's school of discipleship. Where can we learn it, and how? Although it can most certainly be learned by anyone, anywhere, the mission field is a marvelous laboratory for the learning of lowliness and freedom.

Freedom from the control of possessions. Twenty-two years ago, when we first came to Africa, we did our best to avoid this freedom; we brought many barrels of possessions with us. But Jesus is a patient teacher. Gently he took away this item; then he allowed rainwater to spoil that item. This item of cherished furniture was broken in transit; that piece of "necessary" equipment was stolen. The frequent packings and unpackings of "belongings" (do they

Daniel E. Fountain, M.D., is a medical missionary with the Board of International Ministries, American Baptist Churches. Dr. Fountain and his wife, Miriam, are the parents of three children. ©1983 Billy Graham Evangelistic Association.

belong to us, or do we not rather belong to them?) are slowly convincing us of the "blessedness of possessing nothing." We have never been reduced to nothing, and Christ may never bring us to that point. But he is teaching us to commit everything to his control, while graciously permitting us to enjoy so many good things.

Freedom from the control of money. It is commonly reported in U.S. church circles that missionaries are poor. This is untrue. We live among people whose income is perhaps 1/500th of ours. There is no way we can be considered financially poor. So this lesson of true poverty is difficult for us to learn. Perhaps it is more difficult for us missionaries to learn it because we actually enjoy being considered poor by our friends and even come to believe that we are! But Jesus again is our teacher. "The food you gave to the malnourished mother and her child, how much food did you have left? The gift you gave to the pastor to help send his children to school, what did you do without to make that gift possible?" Slowly Jesus Christ is teaching us that true poverty lies not in giving all our money to God, but rather that all the money we have belongs to him. Genuine poverty of spirit and freedom from control of money will come only when Christ has full control of all of our money.

Freedom from the tyranny of time. Another great tyrant of modern life is time. "Make every minute count. Plan ahead. Manage your time effectively. Try to avoid interruptions." (Yes, and try to avoid stomach ulcers, migraines and high blood pressure as well!)

In our busy ministry of health, development, the training of personnel and the building of the Church, time is at a premium; there is never enough. But the Lord said, "My ways are not your ways,"[1] and his timing is most often not our timing. How often he has used interruptions to make this lesson clear, and how often have I failed. A patient wants to ask a question, but the clinic is full of other patients and there is no time. A student has a family problem, but there are too many courses to prepare and to teach. A colleague needs counsel, but the pressures of the hospital, of meetings, of correspondence, rule out the time necessary. And the family? Perhaps when we take our next vacation!

Over and over the Lord has used a neglected patient, a resentful colleague, a disappointed son, to bring home his instructions on the use of time. "If these programs are Mine, why don't you let Me handle them? Which is more important: the programs, or the people to whom I have sent you?"

In Christ's schedule there are no interruptions. The unexpected may occur, but if I plan my time with him, with his objectives in mind, then every seeming interruption is someone or something he has sent for a purpose. And somehow the programs fall into their proper places.

Freedom from clinging to family. "Your children are also mine," says our Teacher. Ouch! That one really hurts! Are we indeed free if we keep possession of our children? No, says the Master, in Luke 14:26.

Twelve years ago we faced the necessity of being separated from our two oldest children; they had to go to boarding school and be away from us for nine months of the year. Who would encourage them spiritually? Who would make sure that they studied properly? Who would see that their teeth were brushed and their fingernails clean? It was not easy to handle that issue, especially as we were aware of the strong spiritual battles in which they were already engaged and the many subtle temptations they would face in school and in the mission hostel. But our loving Lord asked us a question to which only one answer was possible: "Who can best care for your children, you or I?"

So we committed our children into his hands, and how graciously the Lord has proved his faithfulness: loving colleagues in the city became substitute parents; an M.A.F. pilot took our son under his spiritual wing; we had extra opportunities to go to Kinshasa to be with them on special occasions. Our oldest daughter is now a missionary volunteer here in Africa, and our two sons are preparing to serve wherever Christ leads them. Our family is so much closer than we probably ever would have been had we "clung." "And all these things shall be added unto you."[2]

Freedom from self. Possessions, money, time, children—these are tangible. We can count them and can make decisions about them. To release them all to the Lord is difficult and often painful, yet in a sense we can "see" what we have done. Herein comes the most difficult matter of all. What we cling to the hardest, what we resist surrendering to the bitter end, what the Lord must wrestle with us about through the dark night of the soul, is our ego.

How subtle are these egos of ours. "This program is not mine; it is the Lord's." Yet when did I consult him about it and wait for his answer?

"This is not my idea; it comes from the Bible itself." But am I sure that the Lord wants this biblical idea presented at this time and in this way? Have I prostrated myself before him in patient humility to wait for his leading? Most often, no. It has been my ego seeking to accomplish what my wisdom, my common sense, instruct me is right and then using the Bible to hammer it home. Meanwhile the Lord waits.

If my program is rejected by my African colleagues, if my idea is refused, am I crushed? Or perhaps do I rationalize it by assuming that these poor people rejected the Lord's will for them? But in neither case have I learned lowliness, and in neither case is my spirit free. He has made it clear that I must wait first on him. Then through his Spirit he can instruct me in what I am to do and how. He will open the proper doors at the proper time to accomplish his program—see Acts 16:6-10.

One final lesson. In the school of lowliness there is no graduation, no diploma. Classes are held daily and will continue until the final "well done" is heard.

By the side of our home grows a lowly plant. A member of the cactus family, it has nothing attractive about it, just stems and flat broad leaves. But one day, on the side of one of the ordinary leaves, a tiny bud appears. For four weeks this bud lengthens and develops. Then one evening, when the sun has set and other tropical life around it has gone to sleep, the petals open and the night-blooming cereus bursts into one of the most magnificent flowers in all of God's creation. Through the dark night it blooms, emitting its rich fragrance. As the first streaks of dawn light the eastern sky, it bows its head, folds its petals and is finished.

The beauty of lowliness. If I can learn to be God's lowly servant, whether in Africa or in the United States or anywhere else, then he will bring to gorgeous bloom the flower he has put within me. It may be in the dark of the night when no one passes by, but the Maker sees and declares, "It is good."

---

(1) Isaiah 55:8-9. (2) Luke 10:31, KJV

"Gossip? Me?"

Elva Cobb Martin

After becoming a Christian, I soon became aware of a part of my body that refused to become "new." My tongue—my conversation, my talk—often lapsed into its old nature.

Like a chameleon, my words seemed to take on the tone of surrounding conversation, especially gossip.

Yet God's Word had promised I would become a new creature,[1] and I was sure that newness should include my tongue.

What was wrong?

I searched the Scriptures and found my problem defined in the book of James: "The tongue is a fire, a world of iniquity: so is the tongue among our members, that it defileth the whole body. . . . For every kind of beasts . . . hath been tamed of mankind: but the tongue can no man tame."[2]

The dictionary defines a gossip as "a person who habitually retails facts, rumors or behind-the-scenes information of an intimate, personal or sensational nature."

Elva Cobb Martin is a free-lance writer and a homemaker who has written articles for several Christian magazines. She and her husband, Dwayne, are the parents of one son and live in Anderson, South Carolina, where they attend Freedom Life Fellowship. ©1984 Elva Cobb Martin.

One morning I answered my phone after cleaning up from breakfast. "Hello."

"Elva, you've just got to watch the evening news . . ."

Although a warning bell sounded in my mind, I continued to listen as a friend described indictments soon to be made of local persons supposedly involved in a statewide drug ring.

A shadow settled across my day and, later, over my heart. There were no indictments that day or the next, except in my Christian conscience. I had willfully listened to malicious gossip. Whether or not I repeated it, I knew that I would remember it the next time I saw the persons "accused." The doubt thus planted in my mind amounted to a trial without a jury.

I decided to eradicate gossip from my life. The task proved formidable because gossip seems to have become a national pastime — whispering gossip, listening to gossip, reading gossip. For several popular magazines on the newstands gossip is big business; but Christians, Scripture tells us, should "speak not evil one of another."[3]

Why do we slip so easily into the gossip habit? James, in chapters three and four, explains that our tongues are set on fire against our brother by the lust and envy in our hearts. As I worked on my gossip habit, I asked myself some questions: Am I sitting in judgment of my neighbors? Am I jealous of others and secretly wishing to see them put down? Am I trying to raise my own self-esteem by lowering the estimate that I have, or that others have, of another person?

Having begun to root out the reason for gossip, I could ask God's forgiveness and healing. Only he can help me discern and relieve my underlying stress, envy and low self-esteem. I realized I would have to make a covenant with my mouth and ears if I hoped to keep gossip from marring my new life in Christ.

I allowed the gossip of a few of my friends to keep me from making progress at first:

"Listen, have I got something to tell you!"

"Did you hear about Bob and Sue?"

"I hear that Tom's involved in drugs and . . ."

The Christian's exposure to gossip is as inevitable as exposure to bad television programs and cigarette smoke, but I learned to deal with gossiping friends in much the same way that I deal with exposure to bad television. I "switch channels" in our conversations and ask questions about family members, hobbies and goals. In most cases it works.

I sadly found, however, that I have to avoid prolonged company of a few associates. They continue to expose me to gossip no matter how hard I try to change the subject and I am not comfortable where gossip is taking place. One always hates to give up friends, but consolation can be found in an old proverb: "Whoever gossips to you will gossip of you."

An ingrained habit, stopped in its tracks, will leave empty spaces in a person's thoughts, reading and conversation. To prevent gossip's return, I knew that these spaces in my life must be filled. I learned to fill them with the beautiful "whatsoevers" of Philippians: "Whatsoever things are true, whatsoever things are honest, whatsoever things are just, whatsoever things are pure, whatsoever things are lovely, whatsoever things are of good report; if there be any virtue, and if there be any praise, think on these things."[4]

I began to think on them, to select my reading material by them, to inject them into my conversation—the true, the honest, the just, the pure, the lovely, the good reports, words of virtue and of praise. I found that my thoughts, my reading, my conversation, did become different as I adopted these new guidelines! In conversations I began mentally to skim the "whatsoevers" to see if I could inject at least one into each conversation.

Gossip casts shadows; the "whatsoevers" shed sunlight.

What will you inject into someone's day?

---

(1) 2 Corinthians 5:17. (2) James 3:6-8, KJV. (3) James 4:11, KJV. (4) Philippians 4:8, KJV

God does not expect us just to cope with a situation; he calls us to be content.
    —KAREN WELLS

"Loving My Enemy"

Pat Rich

Beatrice was one person in our church choir I found difficult to tolerate. In fact, my feelings for her bordered on hatred.

This dislike spoiled my times at communion because she sat next to me and knelt by my side. I withdrew within myself, away from her, wishing she would leave the choir and never come back. As the months passed, my resentment festered into anger against her.

One Sunday evening our rector preached on loving our enemies. He said that the best way to deal with someone we hate is to pray for him.[1]

I was horrified. How could I pray for someone I despised? That seemed to be an impossibility. But I knew that the Bible said, "With God all things are possible."[2]

That evening, as I prayed, my thoughts were confused. I knew that as a Christian I should not harbor a grievance against anyone. Yet I had deliberately turned my back on someone within my own Christian group. My heart was heavy with disgust at my attitude

Pat Rich is a homemaker and a free-lance writer living in Petersham, Sydney, Australia. She and her husband, Kenneth, are the parents of nine children. They attend All Souls' Luchhardt (Anglican). ©1988 Pat Rich.

toward another human being.

Kneeling by my bed, I asked God to forgive me for my hatred toward Beatrice. I then found I was able to pray willingly for her. I asked God to give me understanding and his love, and to take away my hate.

The following day I was at our local shopping center. There, coming toward me, was Beatrice. On other such occasions I had always avoided acknowledging her. This day I walked up to her and asked how she was feeling.

To my amazement, she burst into tears. I led her into a shop doorway where she opened her heart to me. This woman was not the nasty, unkind person I had believed her to be. Instead, she was someone who begged silently for friendship and understanding, someone who needed assurance and compassion.

Beatrice was full of fear, unable to cope. She needed a friend with whom to talk, a friend to help her in moments of anxiety. Rather than hating her, I found myself loving her with a real, deep concern.

This was the beginning of a wonderful, caring friendship that lasted for more than 20 years. Beatrice's sense of humor was a delight, and her joy in our sharing times is something I will always remember.

We, in the choir, grew to love and understand Beatrice. We came to know that in her cranky moments, she was usually worried and upset about something at home. She didn't mean the nasty remarks that sometimes broke from her lips.

The day came when we realized that Beatrice would not be with us for long. She had been a healthy person, but we noticed her gradually becoming thinner. Her round, jolly face lacked the vitality of earlier years.

Eventually she was placed in hospital where she seemed to fade away. One day I visited her and knew that I was soon to lose a much-loved friend.

As I bent to kiss her good-bye, I took her hand and held it tightly. "I love you," I said softly.

She smiled at me. "I know you do, Pat. I know." The expression in her eyes told me that she loved me too.

I walked away praising God that he had used his wonderful power to take the hate from my heart and to replace it with his love. Because he had done this, I had experienced that "with God all things are possible."[2] Because I had obeyed God's Word and prayed for my enemy, God had given me the joy and friendship of someone precious.

---

(1) Matthew 5:43-44. (2) Mark 10:27, KJV

All of our strength has its source in the God who created us. But there seems to be a special kind of strength that he reserves for us to help us through some extremely difficult times. This can be a quiet sort of strength, such as David seemed to experience. When he fled from Saul, he wrote, "I will cry unto God most high; unto God that performeth all things for me. He shall send from heaven, and save me from the reproach of him that would swallow me up" (Psalm 57:2-3, KJV).

David had a quiet, trusting strength from God who removed his fear.

—EVELYN MYERS

4

Living for God Today

"Just as you received Christ Jesus as Lord, continue to live in him, rooted and built up in him, strengthened in the faith as you were taught, and overflowing with thankfulness."
Colossians 2:6-7, NIV

A Letter With a Ragged Edge

Richard L. Baxter

While lying on a hospital bed and recovering from a heart attack, I read these words: "It is plain that you are a letter that has come from Christ, given to us to deliver: a letter written not with ink but with the Spirit of the living God, written not on stone tablets but on the pages of the human heart."[1]

To me those words were startling, challenging and humbling. Though I was in the hospital, I was there as a letter from Christ, reflecting the glory of the divine Author even though I am subject to human frailty. The very raggedness of my humanity lends credence to the divine authorship, for only God could write a living letter on such improbable material.

A Christian is a loving letter. Love is basic to being Christian. If we love not, we are not. This is not sentimentality or effusive feelings, but good old basic love that reaches out to heal the hurt of the world. Love's simplicity is its attraction; its transforming power is its glory. Love is practical, yet transcendent; earthly, yet heavenly. Love is the essence of the divine Author and permeates the whole of life.

Richard L. Baxter is a retired minister and the author of numerous articles. He and his wife, Nellie, live in Arlington, Washington. ©1985 Richard L. Baxter.

A Christian is a letter of compassion. Having experienced the compassion of Christ for our own lostness, we in turn reach out with compassion for the lost. Compassion enables us to take the hurts of others to our hearts, to feel their brokenness. Compassion is the open door to the healing of the hurts and sin of the world.

A Christian is a letter of forgiveness. Rejoicing in the forgiveness of God for our own sins, we reach out with forgiveness to others. Jesus "came not to condemn the world, but that the world might be saved through him."[2] The Christian needs to sit in the seat of the forgiver. Only as we extend the forgiveness to the world are we recipients of his forgiveness.

A Christian is a letter of mercy. We hate and abhor sin, but with mercy we reach out to the lost to bring them into the Kingdom of God. Mercy finds expression in kindness to the lost and in intercessory prayer to God in their behalf. God's mercy is from everlasting to everlasting. He declares it will never fail, but people can ignore it to their doom.

A Christian is a letter of hope. As I lay in the emergency room that morning, I thought, "This may be it! I may not make it!" I said, "If I don't make it, I want everybody to know I am ready to meet the Lord." Suddenly it didn't matter if I went or stayed. I dropped myself into God's hands and felt at peace.

A Christian is a letter reflecting the glory of the Writer. It is a letter that, despite the ragged edge of our humanity, reflects the glory of him who does the writing.

One evening the young pastor who was hospital chaplain for the week came to see me. We shared for a few minutes about the burdens of the ministry; then we prayed. When we finished, he looked at me with wonder and said, "I came here to minister to you, and you have ministered to me."

All I was doing was being a letter with a ragged edge.

---

(1) 2 Corinthians 3:3, NEB. (2) Cf. John 3:17. The Bible verse marked NEB is taken by permission from The New English Bible, With the Apocrypha, copyright ©1961, 1970 The Delegates of the Oxford University Press and The Syndics of the Cambridge University Press, England

A Christian in the Marketplace

Robert R. Lavelle

Two years ago, when I spoke to the students at the University of North Carolina, I had to be taken to the hospital where I was put in cardiac intensive care. The young doctor who cared for me that weekend asked what I was doing in North Carolina. I told him I had come to give a series of lectures on the Christian in business.

"What do you mean by a Christian businessman?" he asked. I told him that I tried to do business in the light of the commands of Jesus, that I walked with Christ and that I was trying to be a Christlike example in my business dealings.

"Come on," he said. "You have to make a profit like everyone else."

I answered, "Certainly, but I have found that profit comes as a result of serving Christ, and serving Christ means meeting the needs of people."

As business people, being Christian should make us different. The Apostle Paul says, "If any man be in Christ, he is a new creature:

Robert R. Lavelle is executive vice president of Dwelling House Savings and Loan Association and president of Lavelle Real Estate, Inc., in Pittsburgh, Pennsylvania. He and his wife, Adah, live in Pittsburgh, where they attend Grace Memorial United Presbyterian Church. ©1983 Robert R. Lavelle.

old things are passed away; behold, all things are become new."[1]
If you are a Christian, whatever you are doing, you should do it
better. You are free to do it better because Christ has brought you
freedom. You have new sight, new hearing, new values, new
understanding. That means I can't do business as some others do.
My Christian experience on Sunday has to be carried out in the
marketplace Monday through Saturday.

In the United States there are as many as 50 million people who
claim to be born again. If that is true, we are about one-fourth of
the population. Shouldn't we be making a difference in our society?

I call myself a born-again person. Several years ago "The Wall
Street Journal" did a series of articles on born-again people. One
article described a born-again businessman as an impeccable
character who did nothing wrong. But the article concluded by
saying that a born-again businessman does business the same as
everybody else. And I thought, "That is wrong; that should not be."

Scripture supports my perception. Jesus tells us that the great
commandment is to "love God with all your heart, your soul, your
mind and your strength and to love your neighbor as yourself."[2]

In Luke 10:25-37 we read that Jesus responded to the lawyer who
asked, "Who is my neighbor?" To answer him, Jesus told the story
of the Good Samaritan helping a stricken man. The Samaritan had
his eyes open to see the needs of others. Sometimes our eyes are
not open. We see only our own needs and are busy fulfilling them.

Any good humanist can do good things, but a humanist thinks
he can do them in his own strength. I used to be a member of
that group, thinking that I could do good in my own strength.
But any time that helping someone else conflicted with my personal needs I rationalized and helped only myself. I would say,
"It's only natural that I do this." But Jesus said that we can be better than "natural," better than we really are, and that we will do
greater works than he did because of what he did for us. Giving
ourselves to him first helps us to be able to see what we should
be doing for others.

We have an economic rule that says you lend at the highest rate
and borrow money at the lowest rate. But that rule denies both
Matthew 25, where Jesus spoke of serving the hungry, the naked
and the poor; and Luke 10, where Jesus gave the parable of the
Good Samaritan. If we follow strict business rules, then we can't
help the people who have the greatest need—they are the highest
risk and promise the lowest return. These people are not helped

by our normal business dealings.

People reply that we have to be practical. Every time I hear that I think, "Here's another attempt to deny a biblical principle." We hear it said that the business of business is business. When people say that, they are saying that business is different from everyday relationships. I say this is wrong. Business consists of the interpersonal relationships between people.

One writer said that the only function of a corporation is to make a profit for its shareholders, that it has no social function at all. I say that even though a corporation is a legal entity, it is still run by human beings and the corporation must be made to respond to human needs.

We contribute to welfare and look after people that way, but the welfare system perpetuates dependency. What the Christian needs to do is to help the poor person help himself. Someone has said, "If you give a man a fish, he eats for a day. But if you teach him how to fish, he eats for the rest of his life."

I run the Dwelling House Savings and Loan Association, which is located in a poor district. We are there by choice. We try to help people help themselves. It means taking time to teach and counsel and give opportunities to people who would not have opportunities because they had messed up before.

The bank examiners came to our office a couple of years ago, and one who had never been there before looked around and said, "This is a terrible location. What are you doing here?"

"Well," I said, "this is where the people are."

He said, "But these people don't have any money."

"Yes, that's true, but we're trying to change that," I replied.

He thought I was crazy, but after being there 10 days he said, "If what you are doing catches on, it will be like a snowball going downhill."

Only the Christian can do what needs to be done. Jesus said that we are to walk the second mile. We know that the people to whom he spoke were under Roman occupation. A Roman soldier could take any person and make him carry his pack a mile. But the Roman law was just—the soldier couldn't make him go any farther. But Jesus said, "If someone wants you to carry his pack one mile, you carry it two miles."[3]

A person might reply, "Why should I carry it for two miles when I don't want to carry it even for one?" Wasn't Jesus saying that we are to do the things we don't have to do, things we are not required to do? When we come to the end of the mile, we look around and say, "I'll keep carrying it." When the person we are helping asks why we are doing it, then we have a chance to tell him about Christ.

That happens in our business frequently. Recently we were at a closing where we had arranged for a young couple to obtain a mortgage at one per cent below market. The builder pointed out to the couple that that would save them about $7,000 over the years. They asked why I did it. I said, "Otherwise you wouldn't have been able to own a home with all the rights that property owners have, such as income tax deductions and the power to change things in the schools."

"But why did you do it?" they asked.

And that's when I told them about Jesus Christ. Right in the middle of the complex title changes, everyone suddenly felt different. Even the title officer felt different. He said so.

The Christian business person attracts people to Christ by serving need, not greed. When we do something to meet someone's need, he will ask why we are doing it. And then we can tell them that it is because of the love of Christ. No one can be apathetic in the face of God's love—it is the most powerful force there is.

---

(1) 2 Corinthians 5:17, KJV. (2) Cf. Matthew 22:37,39. (3) Cf. Matthew 5:41

Dear Lord, thank You for the dry and barren times of my life that bring me closer to You. For could You satisfy my thirst if it were already quenched? Could You fill me with good things if I already contained them all? Could You grant me the joy, peace and love I long for so deeply if I already had perfect bliss, perfect peace, perfect love? Although the desert can be lonely and dry, I thank You for drops of living water that my thirsty soul drinks; for the bits of food You feed my hungry spirit; for the sweet tastes of peace, joy and love.

    —CAROL SOKOL

Discipline

Richard J. Foster

The disciplined person is the person who can do what needs to be done when it needs to be done. The disciplined person is the person who can live in the appropriateness of the hour. The extreme ascetic and the glutton have exactly the same problem: they cannot live appropriately; they cannot do what needs to be done when it needs to be done.

The disciplined person is the free person. Demosthenes was free to be a great orator only because he had gone through the discipline of speaking above the ocean roar with pebbles in his mouth. George Frederick Handel was free to compose his magnificent "Messiah" only because he had schooled himself in music theory. Joni Eareckson Tada, who is a quadriplegic, is free to bless us with her art only because she was willing to go through the discipline of many painful and discouraging hours of painting, holding the brush

Richard J. Foster, D.P.T., is associate professor of theology and writer-in-residence, Friends University, Wichita, Kansas. He is the author of several books, including "Celebration of Discipline: The Path of Spiritual Growth" and "Freedom of Simplicity." He and his wife, Carolynn, are the parents of two children and live in Wichita, where they attend Northridge Friends Church. ©1982 Billy Graham Evangelistic Association.

between her teeth.

The disciplined person is a flexible person. Rigidity is the first sign that discipline has gone to seed. The rigid person calcifies what should always remain alive and growing. The disciplined person is always free to respond to every movement of divine grace. The Christian disciplines anchor us in God which in turn frees us to be able to hear his voice and to obey his Word.

Jesus Our Model

Jesus Christ is the perfect example of the disciplined person. When the need of the hour was to fast, he was able to fast; when feasting was appropriate, he was free to feast. When teaching was needed, he always had the life-giving message; when silence was appropriate, he had the power to "speak not a word."

In contrast to the rigidity of the Scribes and the Pharisees, Jesus was always responsive to the word of the Father. He was able to disregard "the traditions of men" when the appropriate response was to obey "the word of God." When a perfect sacrifice was needed for our redemption, Jesus was free to despise the shame and become "obedient unto death, even death on a cross."[1] When we see Jesus, we understand that discipline is liberating, life-giving, jubilant.

The March of Biblical Witnesses

Think of Abraham, who disciplined himself against the security of life in Ur of the Chaldees and instead sought a city whose maker and builder was God. Think of Moses, who disciplined himself against the pleasures of sin for a season and sought instead a life pleasing to God. Think of David, who disciplined himself against the harassment of King Saul and waited patiently until his anointing as king became a reality. Think of Jeremiah, who endured the reproach and derision of his fellow countrymen in order to deliver God's Word to them. Think of the Apostle Paul, who "endured hardness, as a good soldier of Jesus Christ,"[2] in order to bring the Good News of the Gospel to the Gentile world. Think of John the Beloved, who saw the glory of the new heaven and the new earth while enduring banishment on the deserted Island of Patmos.

After his famous litany of faith-heroes, the writer to the Hebrews reminds all of us that "it is for discipline that you [have to] endure."[3] Discipline is the reward of endurance, and it is a great reward because it empowers us to obey God.

Discipline in the Marketplace

I have a friend who had a godly desire which conflicted with a perturbing personal problem. The desire was to have more time to minister to college students. The problem was an excessive and undisciplined use of television. In an act of personal discipline he gave away his TV set and invested his energies in human lives. Now he is free to enter into the real human drama because he turned away from the plastic drama of the screen.

I have a student who has set a personal goal of memorizing one-third of the New Testament by the time he graduates from college. He is preparing for the ministry, and this single discipline will no doubt reap vast dividends in his future teaching and preaching ministry.

I know a Christian executive who refuses to look at his mail until after 12:00 noon. Why? Because his creative energies are at their peak in the morning, and he wants to use every moment of that time in the most productive way possible.

Discipline is not meant to tie us down but to set us free. It is not some heavy burden to be endured, but a means of God's grace to release us from ingrained habit patterns of sin.

Without discipline would there have been an Augustine of Hippo, a Francis of Assisi, an Ignatius of Loyola, a Julian of Norwich, a Catherine of Siena, a Teresa of Avila, a Brother Lawrence, a Martin Luther, a John Wesley, a Hudson Taylor? Think of the legacy of spiritual renewal and vitality these men and women have left us simply because, in acts of discipline and dedication, they joyfully took up the cross and followed the Master.

The Divine Synthesis

"Work out your own salvation," declared the Apostle Paul, "with fear and trembling; for God is at work in you, both to will and to work for his good pleasure."[4] Our working out, God working in—that is the divine synthesis.

Real discipline is no righteousness by works, no vain attempt to save one's self. It is a humble act of placing ourselves before God in such a way that he can work into us the righteousness that we so desperately need.

More than any other New Testament writer, Paul held high the banner of salvation by faith alone. And yet Paul took discipline with utmost seriousness: "I pommel my body and subdue it."[5]. . ."I press on toward the goal for the prize of the upward call of God in Christ Jesus."[6]. . ."Endure hardness, as a good soldier of Jesus Christ."[7]. . ."Fight the good fight of faith."[8] These are not the words of a man who scorned discipline.

We would do well to think of the Christian life as the path of disciplined grace. It is discipline, because there is work for us to do. It is grace because the life of God which we enter into is a gift which we can never earn. Lovingly God works his life into us by grace alone, joyfully we hammer out the reality of this new life on the anvil of discipline. Remember, discipline in and of itself does not make us righteous; it merely places us before God. Having done this, discipline has reached the end of its tether. The transformation that comes is God's work.

Our Undisciplined World

In cheerful nonconformity to the tides of popular opinion the Christian calls for self-discipline in the face of self-indulgence. Modern culture has clearly lost both the desire and the ability to check its runaway passions. As a result, it is powerless to break free from the chains of egocentric self-indulgence. We hold the answer to the sickness of contemporary society. The power of Christ working through the spiritual disciplines emancipates us from the tyranny of our egotistical self-indulgence. We are ushered into a new life of unhurried peace and power. As Thomas à Kempis observed so long ago, "True peace of heart is found in resisting passions, not by yielding to them."[9]

---

(1) Philippians 2:8, RSV. (2) Cf. 2 Timothy 2:3. (3) Hebrews 12:7, NASB. (4) Philippians 2:12-13, RSV. (5) 1 Corinthians 9:27, RSV. (6) Philippians 3:14, RSV. (7) 2 Timothy 2:3, KJV. (8) 1 Timothy 6:12, KJV. (9) "The Imitation of Christ," by Thomas à Kempis, Revised Translation, Grosset & Dunlap, Publishers, New York. The Bible verse marked NASB is taken by permission from the New American Standard Bible, ©1960, 1962, 1963, 1968, 1971, 1972, 1973, 1975, 1977 The Lockman Foundation, La Habra, California

A Call to Courage

John Guest

I f you have discovered your dignity in Jesus Christ and you know what your office is as a child of God rather than just as a child of humankind, but you don't have courage to live it and tell it, you are virtually worthless to the world. Because without courage, who is going to know it?

Winston Churchill said, "Without courage, all other virtues lose their meaning." Let me put it this way: courage is the door through which every virtue must walk. And if that doorway is closed, no one is going to discover how God is making you a new person in Jesus Christ.

In Jeremiah 1:6 we read that the prophet made excuses when God called him to speak. Jeremiah said, "I'm only a youth, I don't know how to speak."

But the Lord read right through Jeremiah. His youth was but an excuse; his real problem was that he was scared. God said, "Don't say, I am only a youth; for to all to whom I send you, you shall go; and whatever I command you, you shall speak. Be not

The Reverend John Guest is rector of St. Stephen's Episcopal Church, Sewickley, Pennsylvania, and founder of the Coalition for Christian Outreach. He and his wife, Kathleen, are the parents of three children. ©1983 John Guest.

afraid of them; for I am with you to deliver you."[1]

The greatest failure in the Christian community today is not lack of knowledge, it is lack of courage. God can never bless cowardice, but he can bless courage even when it is misplaced and even if it is ineptly expressed. So in the Bible we read that the Lord encouraged Jeremiah. He said, "Behold, I make you this day a fortified city, an iron pillar, and bronze walls, against the whole land, against the kings of Judah, its princes, its priests, and the people of the land."[2]

I have struggled with the temptation of being a cowardly pastor. Do you know it is no easier to be courageous when you are in a ministry? The greatest problem in the pulpits of our land is not confusion—although there is plenty of that—it is cowardice. Ministers fear to speak the Word of God plainly and with authority.

A student has the temptation to cowardice on his dormitory floor, or back home with parents, brothers and sisters. And when people go to work, the problem of cowardice doesn't go away. Even if you become chairman of the board of a major corporation, courage to live and declare the Christian life will not get any easier. You may think, "When I'm at the top, then I will speak with authority and they will listen to me." Rubbish! By the time you get to the top, chances are you will be so compromised that you will speak very carefully. That is not to put down persons at the top, but I am telling you that no matter what your station in life, to speak the Word of God in an alien culture leads to intimidation. It is threatening.

I love the courage of a man like Aleksandr Solzhenitsyn who, before 15,000 persons at a Harvard University commencement, described man's sense of responsibility to God and society as growing dimmer. He said that all the glorified technological achievements of progress, including the conquest of outer space, do not redeem the moral poverty of the 20th century. And he identified the West's failing with the biblical idea of sin, the self-deification of man.

How can we become people of courage? We gain courage as we are encouraged by others. God told Paul, "Take courage, for you are going to witness to me in Rome."[3] And when Paul arrived in Rome, Christians from the city walked to greet him. In Acts 28:15 we read, "And the brethren there, when they heard of us, came as far as the Forum of Appius and Three Taverns to meet us. On seeing them Paul thanked God and took courage."[4] Even the great Apostle Paul took courage from these few Christians welcoming him. There is a great need for us to be encouragers of one another so that we can go out and change the world.

Let me tell you that it is marvelous that God has given me a measure of courage, because the No. 1 reason I did not want to give my life to Jesus Christ was cowardice. I was afraid of what others would think of me when I became a Christian. My problem wasn't intellectual. I had that worked out. I wouldn't commit myself to Jesus Christ because I was scared of my friends. When I came to know Jesus Christ, I had struggled three years with being a coward. I am convinced that for many who have not opened their hearts to God, the first reason is cowardice. They are afraid of what their friends or co-workers will say about them when they openly confess themselves to be joined to Christ.

When I went to hear Billy Graham at Harringay Arena in 1954, he spoke about nailing our colors to the mast. That is a phrase from the old sailing ship days. Your color was your flag flying from your mast. When the man in the crow's nest saw an enemy ship he would often call to have the color lowered so that the enemy could not spot the color and blow the ship out of the water. When you nailed your color to the mast, you were in effect saying, "Come what may, this is who I am, this is my commitment. And if an enemy ship coming over the horizon wants to try to blow me out of the water that is up to him. My colors are nailed to the mast." Billy Graham said, "I am asking you, those of you who for cowardly reasons have not accepted Christ, to do so this evening." And I did so that evening. Just as God takes mourning and gives us joy and dancing, he took my cowardice and gave me courage.

I ask you to nail your colors to the mast. As God commands us to go into the world and preach the Gospel to every creature,[5] courage is what we desperately need. If your commitment to Christ has been on the wane, let me ask you afresh to be of good courage and redress your life in the presence of Christ and offer it to him.

The Koh-i-noor diamond is among the most spectacular in the world. Queen Victoria received it as a gift from a maharajah when he was a lad. Later as a grown man this maharajah visited Queen Victoria again. He requested that the stone be brought from the Tower of London to Buckingham Palace. The maharajah took the diamond and, kneeling before the Queen, gave it back to her, saying "Your Majesty, I gave you this jewel when I was a child, too young to know what I was doing. I want to give it to you again in the fullness of my strength, with all of my heart and affection and gratitude, now and forever, fully realizing all that I do."

As believers in Jesus Christ, we need to reiterate those words, offering again our lives to Jesus Christ: "I want to give You back my life, Lord Jesus, that I gave You several years ago. I want to give it again to You with gratitude, fully cognizant of all that I am doing."

All the learning in the world will never change anything until it is marching on the feet of courageous people. We will change the world as the Spirit of God fills us with courage and boldness. Will you join me in commitment to lay aside cowardice and take courage?

---

(1) Cf. Jeremiah 1:7-8. (2) Jeremiah 1:18, RSV. (3) Cf. Acts 23:11. (4) Acts 28:15, RSV. (5) Cf. Mark 16:15

"Just two more days until Friday!" I sighed wearily to a co-worker. Somehow I had lost the joy of living one day at a time. I was continually focusing on Friday.

But a nugget from God's Word reminded me to value my time: "Brethren, the time is short" (1 Corinthians 7:29, KJV). Today needs all my concentration, for I might not see tomorrow. Today's opportunities must be used, or be lost forever. Whatever God allows, it is for a purpose. I don't want to miss out on any aspect of what God has for me by wishing away my days. I examined my priorities and shifted them into proper order.

Now each day of the week is special. I still look forward to Friday, but the rest of the work week seems to hold less drudgery. Through God's grace I have been given today. I want to live it for him.

—KATHY GUINN

AIDS, Sex and the Bible

Billy Graham

During the past months we have been desperately concerned about a disease called AIDS. One night on a television talk show a guest told of a Hollywood actor who stepped out
on his wife to pick up a beautiful woman in a bar. He slept with
her that night, only to wake in the morning to find her gone.
Scrawled in lipstick on the bathroom mirror were the words:
"Welcome to the wonderful world of AIDS!" Can you imagine how
he felt?

Hundreds of thousands of people carry the AIDS virus, most
of whom don't even know it. AIDS has emerged as the No. 1 killer
of males between the ages of 35 and 44 in many of the major cities
around the nation. This is changing some of the lifestyles in America. But we have to change more, or we could be a nation in greater
danger from drugs and the wrong use of sex than we are from
an ideology that we are afraid of, or even nuclear war.

It may be a judgment of God upon us. I can't say that for certain, because only God would know that. But something is happening to us, paying us back for our promiscuity and our free way
of life, in which God has certain rules and regulations outlined
in the Scriptures. Or it could be just a warning from God of something worse yet to come.

When I first started preaching, speakers didn't dare talk about sex because everybody became embarrassed. But today you can watch television and see all that is going on—nobody is embarrassed about anything!

The Bible doesn't teach that sex is a sin. Don't misunderstand! Sex is not a sin. It is a gift from God. But when it is misused, it is a sin.

In Scripture there are several stories of Jesus dealing with sexual sin. There was the woman at the well who had had five husbands, and the one she was living with was not her husband. Jesus changed her life.[1]

Or the woman who was caught in the act of adultery: "The scribes and Pharisees brought unto him a woman taken in adultery; and when they had set her in the midst, They say unto him, Master, this woman was taken in adultery, in the very act. Now Moses in the law commanded us, that such should be stoned: but what sayest thou?"[2]

The question I would like to ask is, "Where was the man?" When you read that God set the death penalty for adultery, the man was to be put to death too.[3] In our society we blame the woman but not the man. We talk about the prostitutes. What about the men who hire them?

One day as Jesus was teaching on the porch of the Temple a great crowd gathered. The Pharisees interrupted, dragging the woman taken in adultery. The Pharisees tried to trap Jesus. If he said, "Yes, stone her," that would get him in trouble with the Roman law. If he said "no," that would get him in trouble with Moses' Law. So they thought that they had him.

But Jesus stooped down and wrote on the ground. We don't know what he wrote. I think he wrote the Ten Commandments. The Scripture says that if we break one commandment, we have broken all of them.[4] Breaking the Law of God is called "sin" in the Bible.

Sin will be judged. We will never commit a sin that will not meet us at the Judgment. We are going to come face to face with the sins that we have committed.

Why did God create sex? It has caused so much trouble, as well as happiness and joy. Many ancient and modern writers hold that the body is evil. That is not true. The Bible teaches that God made man, male and female. And having made them, God said his creation was very good.[5]

God has given us sex, first, to attract us to the opposite sex. Second, sex was given for the propagation of the race. Somebody asked me if I believe in sex. I said, "Yes, I wouldn't be here if it weren't for sex." Third, God has given sex to a man and a woman as a way to express their deep and total love for each other. This is why sex is not just for the amusement of playboys. It is a way to say, "I love you, and I love you alone. I give myself completely to you and you alone as my wife, or as my husband." Fourth, it was given as a glorious pleasure in married love. Fifth, it was given so that a man and a woman could express the unity which binds them. The Bible teaches that "marriage is honorable in all, and the bed undefiled."[6]

There is nothing wrong with sex, if we keep God's guideline. The guideline is: "Thou shalt not commit adultery."[7] Fornication is sex before marriage, and adultery is sex with someone other than your spouse when you are married. That is wrong in the sight of God.

One of the greatest gifts that God ever gave us is sex. We have perverted it, misused it. And it has been one of the downfalls of nations and families, creating every kind of problem you can think of. But in the midst of it all, God loves you and is willing to forgive you and change you and give you a new power to overcome that sin.

The word "love" today seems to mean anything—the word is so loosely used. There is a difference between love and lust. There are three Greek words for love. There is "eros," which is sexual love or lust. There is "phileo," or friendship love. And then there is "agape," God's love. In Christ God can take the "eros," the sexual love, and the "phileo," the friendship love, and lift them to a new level. God can give you a love, even in the sexual relationship, that you cannot have otherwise. There is no sexual relationship comparable to two Christians, two believers, who love each other and are married. Others just cannot reach that depth. They cannot reach that joy. Because sex is spiritual as well as physical, there is nothing like it when you have "agape," God's love, surrounding your marriage.

Today sex is being used to sell everything from soap to automobiles. Everything! But it is the wrong kind of sex. Sex in marriage between two believers is an ecstasy and a joy and a peace and a thrill—I feel sorry for some of you who don't know Christ as your Lord and Savior. You think you are having a good time, but you're not.

Why did God say, "Thou shalt not commit adultery"?[7] First, to protect your marriage. If you commit immorality before marriage, it affects your marriage later. Second, to protect your body. Third, to protect you psychologically. Fourth, to protect society. The moral problem can threaten the security of the nation.

What is immorality? The Bible condemns several things: sensuousness, sensuality, lasciviousness, lewdness and reprobation. God does not judge only the actions but the thoughts and the intents of people as well. The Bible says, "Abstain from fleshly lusts, which war against the soul."[8] These are totally depraved people. Their consciences are either dead or seared. And for some of them, it may be already too late. Many have lost the ability to discern between good and evil. "Furthermore, since they did not think it worthwhile to retain the knowledge of God, he gave them over to a depraved mind, to do what ought not to be done."[9]

For young people between the ages of 13 and 18, the No. 1 influence is peer pressure. I want to answer this question: "How can a young person have victory over sex?" I don't think you can—apart from Christ. I believe with Christ you can overcome the temptations.

By the new birth you can have a new nature. That is what it means: "born from above." Jesus said, "You must be born again."[10]

Christ can forgive all the past. And you can know that everything that you ever did 10, 20, 30 years ago, or what you did yesterday, is forgiven.

And when he says forgiven, it means more than what you and I think. It is justification—just as if you had never sinned. What a wonderful thing it is to be totally cleansed. That is the glory of the Gospel. That is the Good News of the Gospel. In spite of our sins, God loves us. He is willing to forgive us. He is willing to change us. He is willing to give us a new power.

The source of our strength: "So then faith cometh by hearing, and hearing by the word of God."[11] "Let this mind be in you, which was also in Christ Jesus."[12] "How shall a young man cleanse his way? by taking heed thereto according to the word of God."[13] Study the Scriptures.

And pray. If you will pray, as someone said, you don't need to worry about much. If you don't pray, you will worry about everything. Jesus said, "Blessed are the pure in heart: for they shall see God."[14] Is your heart pure? Come to Christ and he will make it pure.

In Christ we are to be obedient: "He that hath my commandments, and keepeth them, he it is that loveth me."[15] Paul wrote to Timothy and said, "Flee . . . youthful lusts."[16] Run!

I remember that years ago a man came to me and said, "Billy, I believe that I am a real Christian. But I have the most evil thoughts and fantasies."

I showed him the Scripture: "There hath no temptation taken you but such as is common to man: but God is faithful, who will not suffer you to be tempted above that ye are able; but will with the temptation also make a way of escape, that ye may be able to bear it."[17]

No temptation has ever come to you that you don't have a way to escape. God provides a way to escape, but you have to take that way. Paul wrote to Timothy, "Keep thyself pure."[18]

Saint Augustine, I suppose, was one of the greatest theologians who ever lived. But before he surrendered to Christ, he was a wicked young man. His besetting sin was lust. When he was first convicted of sin, he prayed, "O Lord, make me pure, but not now." Only when he prayed, "Now, Lord," was he purified. "Now, do it now, Lord." And the Lord did it, and Augustine was converted to Christ. Sixteen hundred years ago he came to Christ, and what a change he made in the direction of Christianity.

We all have a disease worse than AIDS, and that disease is called sin. We are all infected, and we all need to be cleansed by the Great Physician. The Great Physician is the Lord Jesus Christ.

You can be forgiven for the past; you can have power to resist sin now and in the future: "We are more than conquerors through him that loved us."[19] We can be conquerors.

There may still be times when you fall. There may still be times when lust enters your heart. There may still be times when evil thoughts come. But there is power that Christ promises through his Holy Spirit. That power can be yours.

I am asking you to come to the Person of the Lord Jesus Christ so that you too can walk with God.

---

(1) John 4:5-30. (2) John 8:3-5, KJV. (3) Leviticus 20:10. (4) James 2:10. (5) Genesis 1:27,31. (6) Hebrews 13:4, KJV. (7) Exodus 20:14, KJV. (8) 1 Peter 2:11, KJV. (9) Romans 1:28, NIV. (10) John 3:7, NIV. (11) Romans 10:17, KJV. (12) Philippians 2:5, KJV. (13) Cf. Psalm 119:9. (14) Matthew 5:8, KJV. (15) John 14:21, KJV. (16) 2 Timothy 2:22, KJV. (17) 1 Corinthians 10:13, KJV. (18) 1 Timothy 5:22, KJV. (19) Romans 8:37, KJV. Bible verses marked NIV are taken by permission from The Holy Bible, New International Version, copyright ©1973, 1978, 1984 International Bible Society, East Brunswick, New Jersey

---

Spiritual Freshness of Life

Michael Green

How are we going to keep fresh? Our soul, says the Scripture, is meant to "be like a watered garden."[1] We are meant to have rivers of living water flowing out of us. We are meant to embody the peace of which we speak. We are meant to be beautiful gardens in the midst of dry deserts. There may be more ways of keeping fresh that God hasn't taught me yet, but here are four I am sure are important.

First, **devotional life.** Ah, we have heard that all before. It goes without saying that our devotional life must be strong. Yes, but that is just the trouble. It does go without saying, and without noticing. It goes! Imperceptibly, we find that we begin to love God's work more than we love God. Imperceptibly, we find ourselves studying just those passages of the Bible that we are going to preach

Michael Green is professor of evangelism at Regent College in Vancouver, British Columbia, and the author of numerous books, including "World on the Run" and "Evangelism in the Early Church." He and his wife, Rosemary, are the parents of four children. This article, ©1985 Billy Graham Evangelistic Association, is abridged from a message given at the International Conference for Itinerant Evangelists, July 12-21, 1983, Amsterdam, The Netherlands. His message is included in "The Work of an Evangelist," a compendium of ICIE material published by World Wide Publications, Minneapolis, Minnesota.

on soon. It is not love for the Word that urges us on; it is the urgency of the need for preparation. Imperceptibly, we find that we are better at applying the Scriptures to other people's lives than we are to our own. Imperceptibly, we find that under pressure our prayer life gets squeezed out—the prayer that is lingering with the Lord—the prayer of adoration and delight in his company—the prayer of simple and single-hearted devotion. That is the thing that goes!

Our Lord looks for first love, so the book of Revelation tells us.[2] Instead he finds everything else. He finds hard work and perseverance. He finds doctrinal soundness and hatred of heresy, but he misses the first love.

Without noticing it, we can become dry shadows of our former selves. If the fresh sap of our relationship with the Lord doesn't flow through the branches of our lives anymore, we are on the road toward hypocrisy, and unbelievers have a very sharp nose for it.

Second, **family life.** Some homes are like pools of light and love—you can just see the love glowing between husband and wife, and the kids are delightful. They are by no means carbon copies of Dad or Mom. They have a freshness and an independence, but they love the Lord, and they are working out a dynamic Christianity in their own modern way.

But we all know the other sort of home where there is deep tension between the partners, where it is not a happy place to be, where the kids have been turned off by the Christian faith. Children need to be loved and loved and loved, loved without strings attached, loved if they don't go to church, loved when they are a pain in the neck. Only in that way can they understand about the love of the Father pursuing them into the far country whether they hear or whether they forbear. We do not make enough time for our children. Instead, we give them presents and hope that will make amends. But it will not make amends. In a busy life it is not possible to spend as much time with a child as we would want, but give them quality time. I take one away with me sometimes to spend a weekend, to concentrate on that one for a weekend. And that carries them for a long time, because it is quality time, and they are made to feel special.

And most important is time spent with your own life partner. One thing I know about my life partner, although she's sturdy and independent, is that my absence does things to her. When I'm away, everybody relates to her, and on my return, they look to me. That is hard. And if I sweep in immediately and head up the household, it is difficult for her to adjust. It is difficult for her to get the feel of what I have been doing. She hasn't been in it. She has had the rough, unglamorous side, while I've been the center of attention. I have made a lot of mistakes in my married life at this point, and I hope that if you haven't, you won't.

Third, **involvement.** It is all too easy to get out of touch with the very people we are trying to evangelize. I think of a situation in Latin America I saw not so long ago where there were a vast number of expatriate missionaries. They did a superb job running a radio station, but they didn't learn the local language. They didn't begin to identify with the local people. God didn't love us so much that he sent radio messages to us. He came himself; he got involved. The Word was made flesh. We need to incarnate our message, and to do so in two ways. We need to use our eyes and our minds. And second, we need to use our feet and our hearts. We need to see the pathways for the Gospel in the ordinary things round about us. "Today is the day of salvation."[3] Our presentation of the Gospel needs to be as fresh as the morning newspaper. We have to be involved and alert to the world around us—its politics, the cries of its pop songs, the agonies of its drama. We have to keep growing. We have to use our eyes and our minds. But we also have to use our hearts and our feet. Two things you notice about Jesus' evangelism. One, it springs from compassion. And two, it concentrates on the poor.

Is that compassion still burning in you? I still find myself sometimes weeping as I lead somebody to Christ. I miss the seriousness, the tears, the suffering, in a lot of modern evangelism. We get a bit professional, we become separated from real people and where they are at.

I was deeply moved by clergy in Uganda going out to work for $60 a year in their ministries, or Bible Society colporteurs going into the terrible encampments in Guatemala City after the earthquake and founding churches in that impossible situation. It is the Third World evangelists who know about identification with people. We Western Christians need to hang our heads in shame. The glory of mission is in those dedicated men and women who hazard their lives for the Lord Jesus and throw in their lot with the poor and the dying and the lowest of the low. And such evangelists have no money. They worry about where the next meal is coming from. They don't know how their children will be educated. But they are the real heroes. And like their Master, their feet follow their hearts. They go because they have compassion. Compassion for the lost keeps us fresh.

Fourth, **body life.** The evangelist needs to belong to a Christian body, a regular local Christian body of which he is an arm. Think back to Antioch where the Gentile mission was born in Acts 13. There was a shared leadership in that church. There was a love between Jew and Gentile that spilled over and led to table fellowship. There was a great deal of informal evangelism. Indeed, that is how the church was born. We are told that it was a church where the leadership embraced black and white and brown people, with vastly different backgrounds, education and nationality.[4] This was the church that sent out the first missionaries, Paul and Barnabas. They evangelized several towns, they trod new paths, and they came back and told the Christians at Antioch what the Lord had done with them.

I believe that has a great deal to teach us. We need to belong to a live, local church and be an arm stretched out from that church. We need to go back into that church and share with them our speaking invitations. We need to be advised by them as to what to accept and what to reject. We need them to commission us with prayer and the laying on of hands as we go forth. We need to report to them as we come back so that we are seen to be not independent operators but an arm of a body stretching out.

And I mean something else by body life. I mean that we must be part of a living Christian body as we go out. As we travel around with the Good News, we are much more likely to stay fresh if we are part of a team. In this way we don't merely talk about the reconciliation Christ offers, we embody it.

I would say to you who are evangelists, you who run the danger, as I do, of being solo operators, make sure you have a peer group, a group of other men and women who are not your juniors but your equals. Gather around you people who will criticize you, who love you, who encourage you, who will pick you up off the floor. Travel with those people if you possibly can. Then I believe you will stay fresh. I pray God it may be so with all of us.

---

(1) Isaiah 58:11, KJV. (2) Revelation 2:4. (3) Cf. 2 Corinthians 6:2. (4) Acts 13:1ff

5

Trusting God Today

"Let us hold unswervingly to the hope we profess, for he who promised is faithful."
Hebrews 10:23, NIV

Trusting Even Without Answers

Jill Briscoe

Have you ever asked God questions and felt you didn't get good answers?

Habakkuk is a man with a lot of questions. For example, Is God there? "How long, O Lord, must I call for help, but you do not listen? Or cry out to you, 'Violence!' but you do not save?"[1]

Have you ever talked with people who are saying things like that?

Recently I spoke with a woman, a grandmother, whose daughter is living out of marriage with a boyfriend. The couple has two children, one of whom was being abused by the father. That grandmother was put into a position of turning her daughter in to the authorities. There's a lot of pain in that situation. That woman said to me in tears, "How is it, Jill, I prayed and prayed and did everything I could! I hammered on the door of heaven. The little three-year-old was still abused. Why didn't God answer?"

Jill Briscoe is a well-known author, a Bible teacher and a speaker. She and her husband, D. Stuart, are the parents of three children and live in Oconomowoc, Wisconsin. She is a member of Elmbrook Church in Waukesha, where her husband serves as pastor. This article is taken by permission from a message delivered at the Evangelical Press Association Convention, May 11-13, 1987. ©1988 Jill Briscoe. This material and more can be found in Jill Briscoe's book "Running on Empty," published by Word, Inc.

These are questions that have to be addressed. So Habakkuk was asking, "Is God there?" and, "Does he care?"

We get the idea that Habakkuk is not getting any answers. Well, he eventually got an answer that he didn't expect and that he particularly didn't want. But this prophet's name means "to embrace." And that's what I want to address: embracing things we don't want to embrace, accepting what we cannot change.

The background to Habakkuk is interesting. Josiah, the good king, has been killed in battle. Jehoiakim is on the throne; he is the bad guy. Habakkuk asks, "God, how is it that the good guy gets killed and the bad guy is sitting on the throne?"

Is God there? Does he care? What about the problem of unanswered prayer? Habakkuk says, "The law is paralyzed"²-the right thing is not done; "Justice never prevails"²-why doesn't God do something?

God gives Habakkuk some answers, and they are the sort of answers that Habakkuk thought he could have done without! God says, "Look at the nations and watch—and be utterly amazed. For I am going to do something in your days that you would not believe, even if you were told. I am raising up the Babylonians . . . "³

The Lord describes the Babylonians (or Chaldeans) as a "ruthless people,"⁴ people who will come like the "wicked foe,"⁵ to catch up the Israelites with hooks, to gather them in their dragnet.⁶ Then the Lord explains that the Israelites will be like a load of fish, mangled in the net of these awful Babylonians.

Habakkuk is absolutely stunned. And he says to God, "First I asked You if You were even there. Then I asked You, 'Don't You care?' Now I ask You, 'Is this fair?' How can You use the unholy to punish the holy?"⁷

Habakkuk loses hope in the fairness and the goodness and the justice of God. When we do that, we are in trouble; we have lost everything. Where are we going to go when we lose hope in the character of God?

In chapter 2, we find Habakkuk feeling guilty for asking all those questions. He decides to "stand at my watch and station myself on the ramparts; I will look to see what he will say to me, and what answer I am to give to this complaint."⁸

When we can't even pray because we feel so bad about our attitude toward God and what he's doing and what he isn't doing, then the only thing we can do is to wait until we see it from his perspective. And that's what Habakkuk wisely does; he waits to embrace God's answer: "I will wait until I see it from Your viewpoint. I will wait until I get Your perspective in order."[8]

God then says to Habakkuk, "The answer to your questions or to your whys is Who. It is I. I am the Answer."[9]

Indeed, God explains that he is working out his purposes. "Write down the revelation. . . . The revelation awaits an appointed time; it speaks of the end and will not prove false. Though it linger, wait for it; it will certainly come and will not delay."[10]

God is saying that the wicked will be punished in the end. And "the earth will be filled with the knowledge of the glory of the Lord, as the waters cover the sea."[11]

The enemy will come and will amass Israel's wealth and rape them of all their money, but the Babylonians will lose all that wealth in the end. They will coerce the Israelites into forced labor, but it will come back on their heads because it will not last forever.

God tells Habakkuk, "This will happen in your day and in your time. There is no escape. The Chaldeans are coming. And you are going to live by faith in the middle of it." That wonderful verse "The just shall live by . . . faith"[12] is in chapter two.

At this point God gives Habakkuk a vision of the Holy One coming from Edom. His glory fills the world, and all nature is convulsed before him and the prophet too.

Habakkuk responds by saying, "I heard and my heart pounded, my lips quivered at the sound; decay crept into my bones, and my legs trembled."[13] What is Habakkuk talking about? Has he seen the Chaldeans? No. He has seen the Lord!

Even though he knows that the Chaldeans are coming and that he cannot escape the invading army, Habakkuk, once he has seen God, is ready to do something about it. He resolves to be faithful forever.

What are our prayers like when we see the Chaldeans on our horizon? Don't we pray to escape them? Don't we say, "God, let them go on to the person next to me. Don't let them overrun me"? Of course we do if we are like most people. That's my first prayer when I see the Chaldeans approaching.

But what do we do when God says we can't escape? How do we embrace a situation that's tough? Are we willing to accept something we cannot change?

"The just shall live by . . . faith."[12] Those who trust in him who is faithful will become like him. Trust produces endurance. And the person who shows his trust in God by his faithfulness to God will find God faithful in keeping him.

Finally we come to the triumphant statement at the end of the book of Habakkuk: "Though the fig tree does not bud and there are no grapes on the vines, though the olive crop fails and the fields produce no food, though there are no sheep in the pen and no cattle in the stalls, yet I will rejoice in the Lord, I will be joyful in God my Savior."[14]

Habakkuk's love for God was not based on what God would give him. Even if God sent him suffering and loss, he would still rejoice—not in the situation but in his Savior.

I had a dear friend who had a terrible battle with leukemia and other forms of cancer. The day she died she called me. I could hardly hear her voice.

She said, "Jill, it's Joanie. I just called to say good-bye." It was just as if she were going on a trip somewhere.

And as I listened, this very, very faint voice said to me, "Well, it's true, Jill. Tell them, tell them it's all true. I'll see you in heaven."

I always remember that because Joanie was somebody who had lived through this whole thing that I've explained in principle. She had asked her questions: Is God there? Does he care? Is it fair?

The Chaldeans were trampling all over her life, and God had said, "This is how it has to be."

I saw her embrace God's answer. God gave her a vision of himself.

---

(1) Habakkuk 1:2, NIV. (2) Habakkuk 1:4, NIV. (3) Habakkuk 1:5-6, NIV. (4) Habakkuk 1:6, NIV. (5) Habakkuk 1:15, NIV. (6) Habakkuk 1:15. (7) Cf. Habakkuk 1:13. (8) Cf. Habakkuk 2:1. (9) Cf. Habakkuk 2:2-3. (10) Habakkuk 2:2-3, NIV. (11) Habakkuk 2:14, NIV. (12) Habakkuk 2:4, KJV. (13) Habakkuk 3:16, NIV. (14) Habakkuk 3:17-18, NIV. Bible verses marked NIV are taken by permission from The Holy Bible, New International Version, copyright ©1973, 1978, 1984 International Bible Society, East Brunswick, New Jersey

A Loaf of Bread and Faith

Marie Campbell

We sat next to the baby's crib in our one-room apartment. He slept quietly.

Our conversation was in whispers. We talked of needing a loaf of bread—for sandwiches to take to work, for a supplement for that evening's meal and for toast at breakfast the next day.

The bread was a staple, a need. At that time we could get a loaf for 25 cents. But a quarter seemed like a piece of gold when we were working our way through school.

"I'll go down and get the mail," my husband said softly as he rose from our studio couch. During the long months of pregnancy, I had slept on that couch, cozied up to my hard-working husband, without feeling the need for a comfortable bed with a mattress. But bread, we needed.

"A letter from Mom and Dad," he said when he returned with the mail. "Well, look at this. A quarter."

It was indeed a quarter. Not $10 or $1 but simply a quarter. Mom

Marie Campbell is a free-lance writer and a teaching assistant at the Freeport Public Schools in Long Island, New York. She and her husband, Dwight, are the parents of two grown children. They live in Freeport, where her husband is the pastor of First Baptist Church (Baptist General Conference). ©1988 Marie Ellen Campbell.

had sent it as payment for a compliment I wrote in my last letter. How I loved her sense of humor at that moment. And I knew again that the Lord was showing us he cared for our needs before we knew we had them. He was always faithful.

Walking in faith is exciting.

◆ ◆ ◆

Lord,
    these are days
    when the
    craftiest hunter and
        trapper around
    doesn't display
        his license or
    sport a glowing orange
        cap and vest.
Sharp and skilled at
        every sneaking device,
he stalks and snares
        the souls of men.
I'd not venture out
        without a prayer
        to keep me
            from the evil one.
And I would ask for
        safe return
        to rest
within my Father's sanctuary.
        —NANCY SPIEGELBERG
        Parma, Ohio

Why Does God Allow Evil?

David M. Scholer

While I served as an interim pastor, a tragedy occurred in the church. A member's 20-year-old daughter was murdered by her husband in her mother's kitchen. He then shot their 18-month-old son (who survived) and killed himself. In the hours that I sat with the grieving mother at the funeral home, she repeated over and over, "God wanted my daughter murdered."

In her grief and despair this woman was attempting to reconcile and maintain what she believed about an omniscient and omnipotent God in the face of evil. We sense immediately that her conclusion is not right; God could hardly have wanted her daughter murdered. And yet, with reflection and sober maturity, we realize how difficult it is to find a better explanation.

Our problem is, "How can a God who is both all-loving and all-powerful allow evil?" Either God is not all-loving or God is not powerful enough to prevent some evils. It is a dilemma, a legitimate theological problem.

David M. Scholer is professor of New Testament and dean at Northern Baptist Theological Seminary in Lombard, Illinois. He is the author of numerous articles and reviews. Dr. Scholer and his wife, Jeannette, are the parents of two children and live in Lombard. They attend First Baptist Church (American Baptist Churches in the U.S.A.) in Oak Park. ©1986 David M. Scholer.

What makes the problem so pressing is that it is not just an in-tellectual mystery; it is also a personal misery. Why does a good man in the prime of life have a heart attack? Why does a young mother die, leaving two small children? Why does an earthquake devastate a city?

We cannot give complete answers to these questions. The questions would not resurface generation after generation if there were what is traditionally called an "answer." Yet, we are forced to say something when someone asks, "If God is in charge of everything, why did he let our friend have a heart attack?" Reflection is important, if only to keep us away from irresponsible thoughts about God that captivate some people from time to time.

These seven perspectives have helped me and others cope with the problem of evil, even if they do not totally solve or answer the problem.

1. God is not ever the author or the cause of evil: "When tempted, no one should say, 'God is tempting me.' For God cannot be tempted by evil, nor does he tempt anyone."[1] Whatever the omnipotence and omniscience of God mean, they do not imply that God causes evil.

2. Sin and evil are real: "If we claim to be without sin, we deceive ourselves and the truth is not in us."[2] In the face of the first assertion, some people have attempted to resolve the issue of evil by claiming that there is no reality to sin and evil. They are only the absence of good or only an apparent reality. This is a delusion. Both experience and history on the one hand and the biblical evidence on the other are stout witnesses to the grim and fearsome reality of sin and evil in our world and in our lives. The biblical affirmation is that sin and evil entered our world through the disobedience of Adam and Eve.[3] And so, all of human history and God's creation are subject to the reality of sin and death, decay and evil.[4]

3. According to biblical teaching, God never promised freedom from pain and evil. The biblical stories are replete with examples, from Abraham to Paul, and of course the Gospel story of Jesus is itself the ultimate confirmation that God never guaranteed deliverance from pain, suffering, abuse or evil. The author of Hebrews points out this reality: "For because he himself has suffered and been tempted, he is able to help those who are tempted,"[5] and, "He learned obedience through what he suffered."[6]

4. God uses, usually in ways beyond our understanding, the

pain of sin and evil—and even sin and evil themselves—for his purposes. This must be the intent of Paul's affirmation in Romans 8:28: "And we know that in all things God works for the good of those who love him, who have been called according to his purpose."[7] Notice also the Lord's response to Paul's experience of a messenger of Satan: "My grace is sufficient for you, for my power is made perfect in weakness."[8] This is another witness to the conviction that God works through the realities of sin and evil.

I think the teaching that we should thank God for everything, even that which is evil, is wrong. It is not *for* everything that we thank God, but *in* or *through* everything, for God is never overcome by evil or sin but uses for his purposes even the tragic realities of human experience. I do not need to understand how God's purposes work out through sin and evil. It is enough for me to embrace the biblical understanding that God does work in and through all experiences.

The biblical witness is clear that among God's purposes for us in the midst of suffering and pain is the molding and strengthening of our character. James wrote, "You know that the testing of your faith produces steadfastness. And let steadfastness have its full effect, that you may be perfect and complete."[9] Challenge, even the challenge of suffering and evil, can provide an unparalleled opportunity for growth toward spiritual maturity.

5. As victims of suffering and evil, we have God's promise of love and comfort. Paul's assertion, "Blessed be the God and Father of our Lord Jesus Christ, the Father of mercies and God of all comfort, who comforts us in all our affliction,"[10] is consistent with the whole biblical witness: God provides comfort and support, love and assurance, to those who turn to him in their pain and suffering.

6. It is hardly appropriate to suggest that evil and suffering experienced by any particular person or group of persons is God's punishment for sin. In the introduction to the beautiful narrative of Jesus' healing of the man born blind, Jesus' disciples asked, "Who sinned, this man or his parents, that he was born blind?"[11] Jesus explicitly rejected the disciples' assumptions and declared that the man's blindness provided an occasion for the good purpose of God to be demonstrated: Jesus is the light of the world![12] Unconfessed sin and unbelief have their due, to be sure, in the biblical teaching, but this is not the answer to the problem of evil.

7. God has provided a triumph! From the beginning of the Bible in Genesis ("He shall bruise your head"[13]) to the final testimony

in Revelation (" 'Surely I am coming soon.' Amen. Come, Lord Jesus!"[14]), the biblical witness is that God will triumph over sin and evil. The decisive blow has been struck! God's victory is given through the Lord Jesus Christ's defeat of death.[15] The reality and triumph of God's raising Christ Jesus from the dead means that tribulation, distress, persecution, famine, nakedness, peril, sword, death, life, angels, principalities, things present, things to come, powers, height, depth[16]–indeed, "nor anything else in all creation, will be able to separate us from the love of God in Christ Jesus our Lord."[17]

These guideposts put us in touch with the realities of God and help us cope with the problem of evil. More than 360 years ago Georg Neumark, as a youth of 20, was robbed on his way to study law at the University of Königsberg. He had to give up his plans to study and wandered for some time as an unemployed, destitute person. Then unexpectedly he found a position as a tutor. On that day young Neumark wrote what has become a well-loved hymn, "If Thou but Suffer God to Guide Thee." It was his expression of thanksgiving for the grace of God in his life. And it was his testimony of trust in God and belief that God will "give thee strength, whate'er betide thee,/And bear thee through the evil days."[18] As we respond to God's call, facing again and again the problem of evil, we too can join together in the affirmation that "God never yet forsook at need/The soul that trusted him indeed."[18]

---

(1) James 1:13, NIV. (2) 1 John 1:8, NIV. (3) Romans 5:12-14. (4) Hebrews 2:14-15. (5) Hebrews 2:18, RSV. (6) Hebrews 5:8, RSV. (7) Romans 8:28, NIV. (8) 2 Corinthians 12:9, NIV. (9) James 1:3-4, RSV. (10) 2 Corinthians 1:3-4, RSV. (11) John 9:2, RSV. (12) John 9:3-5. (13) Genesis 3:15, RSV. (14) Revelation 22:20, RSV. (15) 1 Corinthians 15:54-57. (16) Romans 8:35-39. (17) Romans 8:39, RSV. (18) From "If Thou but Suffer God to Guide Thee," by Georg Neumark, tr. by Catherine Winkworth. Bible verses marked NIV are taken by permission from The Holy Bible, New International Version, copyright © 1973, 1978, 1984 International Bible Society, East Brunswick, New Jersey

Hope

Charles Swindoll

Our bodies have been constructed to withstand an enormous amount of pressure. God has made us to be fairly resilient people. We can survive the heat of the tropics or the icy winds of winter. With undaunted courage we can go through seasons of illness, financial reversals, domestic disappointments, unemployment or the death of someone dear to us . . . if we don't lose the one essential ingredient—hope.

We can rebound against wind and weather, calamity and tragedy, disease and death, so long as we have our hope. And we can live weeks without food, days without water and even several minutes without air, but take away our hope and within the briefest amount of time, we toss in the towel!

Knowing that that is true about his creatures, God calls hope

Charles R. Swindoll is senior pastor of First Evangelical Free Church of Fullerton, California. His daily radio broadcast, "Insight for Living," is aired more than 700 times each day worldwide. Dr. Swindoll is the author of numerous books, including "Killing Giants, Pulling Thorns" and "Growing Strong in the Seasons of Life." He and his wife, Cynthia, are the parents of four children. This article is taken by permission from the booklet "Hope: Our Anchor of the Soul," by Charles R. Swindoll, ©1983 Charles R. Swindoll, Inc., Multnomah Press, Portland, Oregon.

the "anchor of the soul,"[1] the irreplaceable, irreducible source of determination. He calls it our "anchor." "This hope we have as an anchor of the soul, a hope both sure and steadfast and one which enters within the veil, where Jesus has entered as a forerunner for us, having become a high priest forever according to the order of Melchizedek."[2]

Doubts often steal into our lives like termites into a house. These termitelike thoughts eat away at our faith. Usually, we can hold up pretty well under this attack. But occasionally, when a strong gale comes along—a sudden, intense blast—we discover we cannot cope. Our house begins to lean. For some people it completely collapses. It is during these stormy times, during the dark days and nights of tragedy and calamity, that we begin to feel the destructive effects of our doubts.

Maximum Pressure Points

For me, there are three times when the intensity of doubt reaches maximum proportions. One such time is when things that I believe should never happen, happen.

There are times when my loving, gracious, merciful, kind, good, sovereign God surprises me by saying "yes" to something I was convinced he would say "no" to.

I once received a letter from a woman who heard over a radio program a talk that I had given titled "Riding Out the Storm." Little did she know how meaningful it would be to her, for as she was entering into the truth of that message, she arrived at home only to discover that her young, recently married daughter had been brutally murdered. Why did that bad thing happen to that good person? The effect of such termites within our soul is great. They eat away at us and doubt wins a hearing.

Doubts also increase when things that I believe should happen, never happen (the other side of the coin). When I expected God to say "yes," but he said "no."

Joni Eareckson Tada (and thousands like her) trust confidently for a while that the paralysis will go away—that God will say, "Yes, I'll get you through this. I'll teach you some deep lessons and then in days to come, as I heal you completely, I will use you in full health." But God ultimately says "no." When we expect him to say "yes" and he says "no," doubts multiply.

There is a third situation where doubts grow. This takes place when things that I believe should happen now, happen much later.

Of all the doubts, perhaps few are more devastating than those that happen when we are told by God, in effect, "Wait." All of us have wrestled greatly with his timing.

These "pressure points" provide a perfect introduction to the verses in Hebrews 6. This is that great chapter that begins with a strong warning, continues with words of affirmation and closes with words of reassurance and ringing confidence. It addresses the Christian hanging on by his fingernails and he feels himself sliding down the hill. It shouts, "Persevere! Hang tough! Be strong! Don't quit!" Even when God says "no" and you expected "yes." Even when he says "yes" and you anticipated "no." And especially when he says "wait," and you expected it now.

A Classic Example: Abraham

"When God made the promise to Abraham, since He could swear by no one greater, He swore by Himself, saying, 'I will surely bless you, and I will surely multiply you.' And thus, having patiently waited, he obtained the promise."[3]

If you don't know your Bible, you can't appreciate the extent to which Abraham and Sarah trusted God. The two of them had been married for years. God had said to Abraham that in the latter years of his life, his wife was going to have a baby. God promised Abraham in no uncertain terms; he swore on the basis of his own integrity that Sarah would have a son. And then, after making that firm promise, God said, "Now you trust Me. You wait." "In hope against hope he believed . . ."[4]

That's what Hebrews 6 is talking about. "In hope against hope"—when it didn't make sense. When the physical body couldn't pull it off. When it was an impossibility to man. "In order that he might become a father of many nations, according to that which had been spoken, 'So shall your descendants be.' And without becoming weak in faith he contemplated his own body, now as good as dead since he was about a hundred years old, and the deadness of Sarah's womb; yet, with respect to the promise of God, he did not waver in unbelief, but grew strong in faith, giving glory to God, and being fully assured that what He had promised, He was able also to perform."[5]

That's a clear illustration of faith. That's believing even when doubts attack. That's being confident that God knows what he is doing regardless of the waiting period.

While you wait, you give him glory. While you trust him, you give him glory. While you accept the fact that he has you in a holding pattern, you give him glory. Trusting . . . In Spite of the Circumstances.

Abraham is a lesson for us today. The lesson has to do with trusting God when things don't work out our way. This is a lesson on how to deal with doubt. How to have hope when the answers haven't come. How to be confident in God when you cannot be confident in your circumstances or your future.

When the bottom drops out of your life, when hope starts to wear thin, when human logic fails to make much sense, think theologically! Go back and read Hebrews 6:17-18. The theological facts are: (1) there is an unchangeable purpose with God; and (2) that purpose is guaranteed with an oath.

Don't try to explain it all to someone else. You can't. If you could, you would be God. The only thing you can explain theologically is that it is part of his unchangeable purpose, guaranteed with an oath, neither of which is a lie. That's theological thinking. As Solomon stated so well, "[God] has made everything appropriate in its time."[6]

Let me give you a syllogism—a theological syllogism: God is in control of the times and the seasons. Some times are hard and some seasons are dry. So the conclusion is: God is in control of hard times and dry seasons.

We are quick to give God praise when the blessings flow—when the checking account is full and running over; when the job is secure and a promotion is on the horizon; when our health is fine. But we have a tough time believing when those things aren't true.

Benefits come from thinking theologically; you'll see three of them in these two verses in Hebrews 6:18: "By two unchangeable things, in which it is impossible for God to lie, we may have strong encouragement . . ."[7]

Logical thinking will discourage you; theological thinking will encourage you. That's the first benefit . . . personal encouragement.

Read on: ". . . we who have fled for refuge in laying hold of the hope . . ."[7]

That's the second benefit . . . a refuge of hope. Encouragement is the opposite of discouragement. Hope is the opposite of despair. When you accept the fact that sometimes seasons are dry and times are hard and that God is in control of both, you will discover a sense of divine refuge, because the hope is in God and not in yourself.

A strong encouragement and a refuge of hope; for the ultimate benefit, read on: "This hope we have as an anchor of the soul."[1]

That's the third benefit . . . an anchor for the soul. The word "anchor" is used often in ancient literature, but it is used in this way only once in the New Testament, right here in Hebrews 6. Lots of hymns and Gospel songs make use of the anchor metaphor. Every one of them comes back to this verse that refers to the "anchor of the soul."

When you minister to people who have come to the end of their trail because of despair, logical thinking will not help you, nor will it help them.

Human logic breaks down. The mystery is enormous. And it is the enormity of it all that calls for faith. If we could unravel it, why would we need faith? If that were true, all we'd need is the answer in the back of the book and someone to point it out to us; we'd read it and that's all there would be to it. But God's plan is that we walk by faith, not by sight. It is faith and patience that stretch us to the breaking point. Such things send doubt running.

When you find yourself dealing with doubt, remember three things. First, God cannot lie. He can test, and he will. He can say "no," and he will; he can say "yes," and he will; he can say "wait," and he will—but God cannot lie. He must keep his word.

Second, we will not lose. Doubt says, "You lose if you trust God through this." If I read anything in this section of Hebrews 6, I read that in the mysterious manner of God's own timing, for some unexplainable and yet unchangeable purpose, those of us who trust him ultimately win—because God ultimately wins. God cannot lie. We will not lose. Your mate has walked away from you, an unfair departure—you will not lose, child of God. Your baby has been born, and for some reason he or she has been chosen to be one of those special persons on this earth. You will not lose. You've waited and waited, and you were convinced that things would improve, yet things have only gotten worse—keep remembering, you will not lose. God swears on it with an oath that cannot change. You will not lose.

Third—and I guess it's the best of all—our Lord Jesus does not leave us. To quote from Scripture, he "sticks closer than a brother."[8] "Jesus has entered as a forerunner for us, having become a high priest forever."[9]

That means he is there at any time . . . and always.

It is possible that you are thinking thoughts that you have never entertained before, and you're thinking them more often and more seriously. Without trying to use any clichés on you, I would say that this hope Christ can bring, this "anchor of the soul," is the only way. I have no answer other than Jesus Christ. I can't promise you healing, nor can I predict that your world will come back right side up. But I can promise you that he will receive you as you come in faith to him. And he will bring back the hope that you need so desperately.

---

(1) Hebrews 6:19, NASB. (2) Hebrews 6:19-20, NASB. (3) Hebrews 6:13-15, NASB. (4) Romans 4:18, NASB. (5) Romans 4:18-21, NASB. (6) Ecclesiastes 3:11, NASB. (7) Hebrews 6:18, NASB. (8) Proverbs 18:24, NASB. (9) Hebrews 6:20, NASB. Bible verses marked NASB are taken by permission from the New American Standard Bible, ©1960, 1962, 1963, 1968, 1971, 1972, 1973, 1975, 1977 The Lockman Foundation, La Habra, California

Today when I descend the curving route home, I see tiny wisps of mist rising here and there from below the surrounding hills. Rising effortlessly and silently, the mist will become part of something greater, part of a great plan. Ever in motion, moisture comes into our lives as gentle raindrops, pounding surf, blanketing snow, gurgling streams and fluffy clouds. The moisture does not choose how it will rise or fall, whether it will remain in the lowlands or lose itself in vast, towering clouds. It is directed by the Father.

Our lives too are controlled by his hand. As Christians, we can see his hand reaching out in blessing, although when we are called to rise or fall, we may not see the reason. When we trust in God, we can know that what he is doing is for our good and can accept the changes life brings.

—PHOEBE BELL HONIG

Seasons of Waiting

Gail L. Jenner

I t's a blustery autumn day. Somber clouds hang low and leaves cover the yard. As I look out, past the yard fence and across the 80-acre field beyond, I study the dark plowed furrows which stretch from one end to the other. At the end of the last furrow there is a tractor, its big wheels turning. It moves across the landscape tilting and tipping as might a vessel upon a rolling sea.

I have to smile because not always did I view this scene in joyful anticipation. During the first years of our marriage, as farming season overtook us, I would often look out across the barren land in frustration. Indian summer days meant long hours, day after day, even into the night, and I watched my husband from afar as he plowed each field.

"How can you stand it?" I had to ask. "Hour after hour. Don't you get frustrated digging up the same fields every year?"

He smiled. "We have to plow if we are to have a good crop. If I don't take time now, we won't have a harvest next summer."

As a Christian I struggled during the seasons of waiting. When

Gail L. Jenner is a homemaker, a free-lance writer and a high school English teacher. She and her husband, Douglas, and their children live in Etna, California, where they attend Scott Valley Berean Church. ©1987 Gail L. Jenner.

would I see the results of my prayers? When would things change? Didn't God hear me? It was hard to see the blossoms when the trees were bare.

Now I understand that time is the essential element in any growing experience. We don't see that insignificant kernel of wheat growing beneath the dirt, but we know that with time, the seed will grow.

Like my farmer-husband, we Christians are never finished planting and seeding the waiting lives around us. It takes time to sow precious seeds of hope. Whether through discipling, encouraging, serving or nurturing, we are farmers for Christ. And farmers know that with the proper investment of time and work, seeds grow and blossom.

I thank God for my husband who can see bushels of grain in a barren and brown field. As I watch the big tractor dip beneath the horizon, I am reminded again and again that only seasons of waiting bring seasons of harvest.

When will I see the results of my prayers? In time.

Though the wisdom of Providence has ordered you a lower and poorer condition than others, yet consider how many there are that are lower than you in the world. You have but little of the world, yet others have less. . . . If God has given you but a small portion of the world, yet if you are godly he has promised never to forsake you (Hebrews 13:5). Providence has ordered that condition for you which is best for your eternal good. If you had more of the world than you have, your head and heart might not be able to manage it to your advantage.
    —JOHN FLAVEL

From "The Mystery of Providence," by John Flavel, first published 1678; The Banner of Truth Trust, Edinburgh, Scotland, and Carlisle, Pennsylvania, 1963

"Out of My Brokenness"

Norma C. Sanders

Time seemed to stand still as I paced the floor. Blackness enveloped me. Earlier that night my husband had sat across the table from me, his eyes averted. Finally he said he must leave, that he had some thinking to do. I knew something was desperately wrong but could only wonder about the extent of the problem.

The next morning when I asked the reason for his leaving the night before, he threw a bombshell at me. It touched every part of my being and left me shattered. He explained that he was leaving me because he had fallen in love with a young mother who attended the church we were pastoring. My world crumbled; and I seemed to be standing in the midst of an earthquake.

We had survived so many crises together—financial, family problems, major surgeries. How could my husband walk away from all the memories of things we had experienced together?

When I told one of our daughters that her father had chosen another woman, she simply stared at me and replied, "Dad?" That one word spoke volumes. Our three children were grown, but like

Norma C. Sanders is a free-lance writer. The mother of three children, she lives in Sandborn, Indiana, and attends Sandborn Baptist Church (American Baptist Churches in the U.S.A.). ©1987 Norma C. Sanders.

young children in broken homes, they have suffered also. They have experienced a gamut of emotions, beginning with shock and disbelief. The tragedy that could never happen to our family had happened.

During the next weeks, when I worshiped in our church and listened as a supply minister filled the pulpit where my husband had stood, my eyes filled with tears. Watching a couple as they looked lovingly at one another reinforced the fact that I was now alone.

But an ever-present God and loving friends carried me through the aftershock. I was filled with an incredible peace and joy. Some thought that I needed to release my emotions. Yet God's hands seemed to be drying my eyes before the tears had an opportunity to form.

I wondered how I would support myself. I had never been employed outside our home; for 27 years I had enjoyed being a full-time wife and mother to our three children. Now I was faced with the necessity of seeking employment. I asked myself, "What shall I do? Where will I turn?" I was living out in the country without transportation. If I did find employment, how would I get to work? Through all of these questions and many others, God was quietly and wondrously working. His plans for my life as a single woman were slowly evolving.

One day a friend from our former church came to visit with news about a possible job. Her daughter was secretary at an organization which was seeking telephone recruiters for a one-month period. My friend asked if I would be interested.

"Vee," I replied, "I believe God has sent you to tell me this—I would like to apply for the position." I applied for and was given the job. The office was located 35 miles from the parsonage where I was living at the time. I was still without transportation. Then, the day before I began my temporary work, I was given a car.

It was quite an experience rising early in the morning and driving 35 miles to a large city. My driving time was spent singing praises to God who loved me so much—my heavenly Father and my Friend.

Day after day I sat at a telephone, recruiting workers. The work at times was frustrating and tiring, but it was a stimulating experience. I was on my own, yet I was never alone, for God's presence surrounded me; his Spirit was in me and around me. I seemed to feel his gentle touch.

I needed to talk during those days and weeks after my husband left. So many emotions were bottled up inside me; talking was my way of releasing my frustrations. One dear friend phoned every evening after I returned from work. She patiently listened as I asked questions and related unending details of my new job.

One-and-a-half weeks after I began work as a recruiter, the secretary resigned her position. She asked if I would be interested in applying for the job. That night I toiled over a résumé, and prepared for an interview with the supervisor the next morning. Instead of listing places of employment, I wrote of the experiences and skills I had gathered throughout my years of homemaking and serving as a minister's wife. The next morning I prayed silently as I answered the supervisor's questions. I was hired as a district secretary of the nationwide organization.

One of my responsibilities is to counsel people who have heartbreaking problems. God is using my brokenness to serve not only himself but also others.

More than four years have passed since that long, lonely time when I felt that my entire life was over. I thought that I had arrived at my road's end. In reality, it was not the end but a turn which brought me to a deeper commitment to God and his leading. From the beginning I claimed Romans 8:28: "And we know that God causes all things to work together for good to those who love God, to those who are called according to His purpose."* I clung to this promise during the months that followed. There were moments when I didn't understand how God could possibly bring good from the heartache I was experiencing. Now, as I cast a look over the past four years, I can see many ways in which God fulfilled and continues to fulfill the promise of Romans 8:28 in my life.

God is giving me the privilege of sharing his love with others through our denomination's lay witness program. God has brought people struggling with heartaches into my life, and I have had the opportunity to offer encouragement. To them I can offer a cup of cold water in Christ's name.

I am also pursuing a gift of writing. There were times when I allowed bitterness to control my thoughts, actions and words. But God's Holy Spirit didn't permit me to dwell on these negative emotions. Most of my days have been bathed with joy and a deep inner peace.

God continues to fulfill his promise to bring good out of bad, to give strength when I am weary, to provide ways that I might use the talents he has given. Through his loving grace I have discovered new strengths in me.

I know that God's will is that marriage be a lifetime commitment. But when that option is closed, there is yet hope. In God's love I can still be a vital Christian, living a full life and sharing his love with others who need encouragement. God does give victory to overcome discouragement and depression and he does give meaning to life. I know this is true.

---

*Romans 8:28, NASB; taken by permission from the New American Standard Bible, ©1960, 1962, 1963, 1968, 1971, 1972, 1973, 1975, 1977 The Lockman Foundation, La Habra, California

◆ ◆ ◆

Teach us, Lord, true faith.
    When storm winds
howl around us and tornadoes
toss us violently off course,
spinning our lives like
dervishes without a cause,
teach us to trust in You.
Teach us to wait,
    to praise,
    to hope,
that paths ahead,
prepared with sunlight,
will open up and lead us
    where You wait,
into Your Kingdom's pastures,
green and flower-studded,
    rich with peace.
        —LEILA DORNAK
        Oakland, Texas

©1983 Leila Dornak

6

Giving All to God Today

"Whatever you do, work at it with all your heart, as working for the Lord, not for men."
Colossians 3:23, NIV

Candelabra

Marianne Farrin

T he year was 1968, a time of fast expansion for American business overseas, and our young family was in the Philippines,
where my husband was on assignment for his company.

That year was also the turning point in my own personal life.
I was a Christian, but then I began to read the Bible regularly,
underlining many passages.

As I searched the church library for books, I came across "A Man
Called Peter: The Story of Peter Marshall," by Catherine Marshall.
I took the book home, and soon I grew to admire this person and
his enthusiasm for God. I identified with his background as I also
had come to America as an immigrant. I wanted to become like him.

For me, one thing stood out about Peter Marshall's story: his
dependence on God for all his material needs. I became aware
of tithing as a principle of God having control over our pocket-
books. Peter Marshall had come from Scotland with just enough
money in his worn, brown leather billfold to last two weeks; yet

Marianne Farrin is a homemaker and a free-lance writer. She and her husband,
James, are the parents of five children and live in Wyckoff, New Jersey. The
Farrins attend Fardale Trinity Church in Mahwah, New Jersey. ©1985 Marianne
Farrin.

he steadily tithed his small salary.

I took my cue from this story of God's faithfulness. If I were to grow closer to God and to receive all his blessings, I needed to tithe too. Secretly I made a vow to the Lord that 10 percent of my weekly household allowance would henceforth be his.

A few days later I was browsing in an antique shop when I came across a lovely Chinese candelabra. We had moved from Hong Kong the year before, and while in Hong Kong we had acquired Chinese rosewood furniture and a handsome Oriental rug. A glass coffee table allowed the design and colors of the rug to have their maximum effect. We were delighted with our "Chinese" living room. The brass candelabra would complement it perfectly. But where would the money come from? My husband and I managed on a fairly strict budget, keeping up with the lifestyle of the American community around us.

Then I remembered the "tithe," my first tithe which had carefully been set aside in a special compartment of my pocketbook. "The Lord won't mind," I reasoned with myself. "I'll start tithing in a couple of weeks instead." Confidently I approached the shopkeeper about the candelabra. Would she be willing to take half the payment this week and the rest the next week? The woman agreed to those terms, wrote out a receipt and kept the candelabra for my return later.

I walked out, pleased with my purchase, and pictured how nice the candelabra would look on our coffee table, perhaps with red candles.

The week passed quickly, and I returned to the antique shop, one stop among several morning errands. I approached the clerk with the receipt and money in my hand. She disappeared into the back room for what seemed like an unusually long time. I browsed around, admiring the many Oriental artifacts.

Finally she returned, but empty-handed. "I am sorry, but I am not able to sell you the candelabra."

"But why?" I questioned.

"The owner of the shop came by and decided to keep that candelabra for herself and it is no longer for sale. You may choose anything else in its place or take your money back."

Then it dawned on me what I had done. God's portion, God's tithe, had been used for the down payment. The tithe was his and not mine to spend. He was teaching me his ways gently but firmly. With awe and wonder I recognized his hand at work in my life.

With a sense of reverence I placed the tithe in the offering plate the next Sunday.

Several years later, during my devotional Bible study, I came upon this verse in Leviticus: "Nothing devoted, nothing that a man has set apart to the Lord of everything he has, . . . shall be sold or redeemed. Everything devoted is most holy to the Lord."* Carefully I underlined that verse and wrote "candelabra" in the margin. It explained the sacredness of the vow made to the Lord so many years before, a vow he had not allowed me to break for my own growth and his glory.

I have learned many other lessons about obedience to God, but this particular early lesson will always be the milestone in which I learned to give to God what is rightfully his.

---

*Leviticus 27:28, Berkeley; taken by permission from The Holy Bible: The Berkeley Version in Modern English, copyright © 1958, 1959 Zondervan Publishing House, Grand Rapids, Michigan

The truth of God's faithfulness is absorbed through times when life demands more than we think we have to give. God calls us to such a life. His call may mean the foreign mission field where the adjustment to a different culture seems more than we can make. His call may involve witnessing to colleagues in the office which may present a greater risk than we are willing to allow. Or his call may mean further education, the financial cost of which seems more than we can pay. The road to which God calls varies with the individual. Whatever direction, we can be certain that it will be a challenge to us, and we will be tempted to take matters into our own hands and travel a different route. Nevertheless, his chosen path is for our good. It is in following his travel plan that we will move from trust in ourselves to trust in God.

—WARNER DAVIS

"Rest"—God's Word to Compulsive Workers

Robert W. Dickson

O n a scale of one to ten I think I rate a two in the relaxation department. I am a duty-bound, work-oriented product of the tough-time '30s. Work is my middle name. For years my wife and daughter have been urging me to unwind more often.

Every time I study the Word of God, I am struck with the magnitude of the job God has given us Christians. The commands of our Lord to be "salt" and "light," to "go into all the world" and to "be my witnesses"[1] are for doers, not for dreamers. And does not the word "commitment" suggest round-the-clock witnessing, prayer, study of Scripture and church activity? Rest sounds like something the devil invented to keep believers from doing God's work. Besides which, if we are in the Last Days before his return (and we may well be), can we afford to take a day off for fun and recreation, let alone a couple of weeks?

Do you know how I usually justify a vacation? I sandwich it in between a couple of working conferences or church business meetings. For example, soon my wife, Gloria, and I hope to travel to

Robert W. Dickson is senior pastor of Hope Presbyterian Church in Richfield, Minnesota. He and his wife, Gloria, are the parents of two children and live in Minneapolis. ©1983 Billy Graham Evangelistic Association.

the West Coast. Is it for "R and R"? She wisely feels it should be. But does her best friend and sweetheart of 30-plus years agree? No, he tells himself and others, "We have two evangelism meetings to attend. Oh, we may work in a few days just to rest." My Calvinistic, work-ethic background makes me uncomfortable with just unwinding and enjoying the ocean. I will probably carry a briefcase full of church business with me. That way my conscience will get salved while my flesh will keep sagging.

Mercifully for all of us Christian workaholics, Mark was led by the Holy Spirit to record that "take it easy" episode in his account of the Gospel. Read and reread Mark 6:30-32. Put your name in verse 30 where it speaks of "apostles" returning to tell Jesus all they had done and taught. What did the One who "rested" after the "days" of creation say to work-weary men? "Come away by yourselves to a lonely place, and rest a while."[2]

Did those men argue with Jesus? Perhaps a few of them did. Compulsive workers are not limited to the 20th century. But this was the Master reminding them of their humanity. Jesus knows that "new life in him" does not mean superhuman life. Followers of Christ, whether they wear sandals or loafers, get drained out. The Christian walk saps the energy of the best and strongest of servants. Until we receive our resurrection bodies, the flesh and blood that limits us requires an occasional change of pace. Thankfully, the apostles listened to Jesus: "And they went away in the boat to a lonely place by themselves."[3] How very wise to listen to Jesus.

Jesus took the sense of guilt out of rest and relaxation. Didn't he go off to a solitary place for prayer now and again? Frankly, the Savior more than likely also took time out for relaxation too. While being fully God, the Word reminds us that Jesus was also fully human, though sinless.

Years ago a pastor-friend exemplified for me the proper ebb and flow of life. He was a good model. He still is. Bill learned to play as well as pray. He could relax as well as relate the Gospel to life. Gloria and I worked in his Los Angeles church the summer of 1950. His style of life and ministry impressed us. He managed to accomplish quite a bit each week. His sermons were sound and interesting. His people reflected his upbeat love for the Lord. Yet Bill always found time to unwind. It was fun being a part of his staff.

What sticks in my mind is that even when my friend relaxed, the Lord always held a central place in his thoughts. Between games of volleyball, he would quiz us on Bible verses. "Bob, tell us what Philippians 4:6-7 has to say about anxiety." When I didn't know, I would look up the passage and begin to consider its meaning. He enjoyed teasing people good-naturedly. Yet all the while we were learning, praying and feeling good about the whole experience with God. Bill taught me that life in Christ can be delightful and not a drag.

I am reminded of one more lesson my pastor-pal taught me. When Bill took a day off or went on vacation, he usually changed the whole pattern of his daily routine. For example, he drove a delivery truck on his days off. He obviously believed that his mind needed to focus on something other than sermons, pastoral calls and counseling sessions for at least 24 hours a week. Then too I am sure that Bill's ministry benefited from the fact that he could identify with truckers and others in his congregaton who were engaged in secular vocations. Maybe driving a truck one day a week helped him to communicate Christ more effectively. What Paul was to the tent-making business, my friend was to the delivery trade.

What practical steps then may you and I take to rest and relax in such a way that we experience Jesus' abundant life? I propose the following:

Learn to rest in the Lord. Until Jesus becomes the spiritual haven for our lives, we can have no rest from the storms of sin that batter the unprotected soul. The salvation made possible only through faith in Christ relieves us of the restlessness that attends a religion of works. Rest for the soul here and hereafter is all of grace.

Reject Satan's lie that God is pleased only when we are doing something the world might dub "religious." Some church work, as a respected friend of mine likes to say, is not the true work of the Church. God likes to see us concentrate on just being now and again. If a walk around the lake or a quiet pondering of a sunset helps unravel the tangled threads of one's emotions, the rest that results may enable one to serve God far better than frantic activity in his name.

Jesus says it is all right to rest and relax. He advised his disciples to get away from it all. He did himself on occasion. Guilt about unwinding comes from the enemy, never the Lord.

Honor the Lord by the spirit you bring to your times of play. You are Christ's person on the tennis court or golf course as much as you are in the sanctuary or at a Bible study. While a little healthy competition may be acceptable, "playing for blood" does not exactly reflect the word the Apostle Paul gave to the Philippian believers about "doing nothing out of selfish ambition" or "considering others better than yourselves."[4] Unless you are playing for a professional athletic team, you don't have to win to have a wholesome diversion.

Take regular times away from the normal routine. Even short breaks during the day help the flesh recoup so that the spirit can maintain itself. A few calisthenics or a short walk around the office helps clear the cobwebs and offers a quick pick-me-up to the body. As my administrative assistant and secretary know, on those long, tedious work days which begin early and end late, I look for opportunities to take a brisk walk around the block. Often I find that the Lord clears my head and cleanses my spirit with a little jaunt. It is amazing too how watching children at play can help restore one's own childlike spirit.

Stop and smell the roses. To paraphrase Ecclesiastes 3, there is a time for activity and a time for rest.

---

(1) Matthew 5:13, RSV; Matthew 5:14, RSV; Mark 16:15, RSV; Acts 1:8, RSV. (2) Mark 6:31, RSV. (3) Mark 6:32, RSV. (4) Cf. Philippians 2:3

Time:
You Will Never Live This Minute Again

Billy Graham

E very morning we have 86,400 seconds before us to spend and to invest. Each day the bank named "Time" opens a new account. It allows no balances, no overdrafts. If we fail to use the day's deposits, the loss is ours.

Tomorrow will be a glorious and marvelous time for those who live in the will of God and take advantage of every moment and every second that God gives.

I speak at universities, and if I tell young people that time is short, that life is brief, they don't believe it. The Scriptures tell us that life is very brief.

Time is collapsing on us. World War III clouds are gathering on the horizon. If ever there was a time when men and women are trembling with fear and hearts are failing with perplexity, it is now.

Our philosophers are writing stories and articles about this perplexity all the time. We are not finding fulfillment and happiness. What is wrong?

Man is the same right now as he was in Jeremiah's day: "The heart is deceitful above all things, and desperately wicked: who can know it?"[1] Wherever I go throughout the world, I find that man is the same. Whether I am preaching in the Soviet Union, or preaching in Korea, or preaching in Mexico, or preaching in the United States, man is the same.

I don't have to change my messages. I don't have to adapt and become relevant. When I preach the Gospel, I am relevant. The more we try to become relevant, the more irrelevant we become. We don't have to have a new jargon. Just preach and proclaim the Gospel. It has its own built-in power.

The great communicating Agent of the Gospel is the Holy Spirit: "Salvation is of the Lord."[2] The Holy Spirit is the One who does the convicting. He is the One who regenerates. He is the One who baptizes. It is the work of the Holy Spirit. It is up to us to be faithful in our witness.

First is the brevity of time. "Behold, thou hast made my days as an handbreadth; and mine age is as nothing before thee."[3] "A thousand years in thy sight are but as yesterday when it is past, and as a watch in the night."[4] "One day is with the Lord as a thousand years, and a thousand years as one day."[5] Like the grass we spring up, and like the grass, we are mowed down.[6] "My days are like a shadow that declineth; and I am withered like grass. But thou, O Lord, shalt endure for ever; and thy remembrance unto all generations."[7]

God is "from everlasting to everlasting."[8] He never had a beginning; he will never have an end. My mind cannot comprehend that, because I am attuned to time and space.

Each of us has been given the same amount of time—1,440 minutes a day, 168 hours a week. "The days of our years are threescore years and ten; and if by reason of strength they be fourscore years, yet is their strength labor and sorrow; for it is soon cut off, and we fly away."[9]

So, "What is your life? It is even a vapor, that appeareth for a little time, and then vanisheth away."[10]

Second is the urgency of time. The Bible says, "[Redeem] the time, because the days are evil."[11]

Somebody asked me if I had my life to live over again, what would I do? If I knew that Christ was coming tomorrow, do you know what I would do? I would do just exactly what I am doing now. What would you do? If you are in the will of God, faithfully doing what he assigned you to do, you should go right on, right to the moment of his appearance, faithfully doing what he assigned you to do.

Third is the tyranny of time. It controls us, and we become frustrated, running from one thing to another because we do not feel that we have enough time to get everything done that needs to be done. In the Lord's work there is so little time, and so much to do!

Oh, if we could only be like the Lord Jesus, who moved with such serenity! He never seemed to be in a hurry, yet he only had three years of ministry. Jesus said, "As long as it is day, we must do the work of him who sent me. Night is coming, when no one can work."[12]

He taught us that the quality of life is more important than the length of life. To the world, when he was on the cross, he must have seemed a failure. Yet at the end of his life he said, "I have finished the work which thou gavest me to do."[13]

You may not live long, but finish the work God gave you to do. That is the important thing—not to live a long time—but to have a quality of life every day in prayer, the study of the Word, witnessing, bearing the fruit of the Spirit, utilizing the gifts of the Spirit.

When Jesus died, people still needed to be healed, hungry people still needed to be fed; he didn't heal or feed them all. Jesus healed those people who came across his path, and he fed those who were hungry.

You see, the main thing with Jesus was the cross and the resurrection. He realized that man's eternal salvation was far more important than just his body. To the paralyzed man who was brought before him, Jesus didn't say "be healed" first; he said, "Thy sins [are] forgiven thee."[14] I would rather have my sins forgiven.

I have heard Joni Eareckson Tada say many times, "It was worth being paralyzed to know that my sins are forgiven and I'm going to heaven." I have heard many people say that, people who were sitting in wheelchairs or lying in beds.

Time can be our tool, but also we can be its slave. Your life should be committed to certain priorities. Have you sat down and written out some priorities for your life? Your life ought to be carefully planned. Ask the Holy Spirit. Start going to a little place of your own where you meet God alone in prayer. Take a pencil and paper along and write out some things that God says to you.

"[Redeem] the time."[11] The time is urgent; don't waste it. This minute that we are now living will never be lived again. This hour will never be repeated. It will be in the history books in heaven. Your thoughts will be recorded; your actions will be recorded; the decisions you make today will be recorded.

Time calls for immediate action. The fact that time is short calls for us to do something about it. The Scripture says, "Now is the accepted time."[15] Things you ought to do, do now. The family that needs you, spend more time with them now. Write that letter now that you have neglected. Study now. Money you ought to give, give now. Debts you ought to pay, pay now. People you ought to witness to, witness to them now. Every time the clock ticks, it's saying, "Now, now, now!"

"Today if you will hear his voice, don't harden your hearts."[16] Even believers can harden their hearts and lose their sensitivity to the Holy Spirit, who speaks to us sometimes about little things.

I remember when I started preaching. I was in a little church in Florida where 40 or 50 people were present. My father had given me a wristwatch when I graduated from high school; it had a gold band, and I remember I looked down, and it shone in the light. I saw a couple of people looking at it. The Lord said to me, "Take that off. It's distracting."

I said, "Lord, I can surely wear a wristwatch that my daddy gave me." But it was sensitivity that God was teaching me—to be sensitive to the little things. I took it off and put it in my pocket. I never wore it in the pulpit again. God was teaching me a lesson about even little things, that I am to listen to the voice of the Holy Spirit.

Then there is the warning of time. Time is running out for all of us. Be sure that you have given your life to Christ. Ask Jesus Christ to be your Savior and Lord. Time is too short for indecision and vacillation. Don't halt between two opinions. "And Elijah came unto all the people, and said, How long halt ye between two opinions? if the Lord be God, follow him: but if Baal, then follow him. And the people answered him not a word."[17]

Give your life to Christ now. Don't wait. "Now is the accepted time; . . . now is the day of salvation."[15] Then every day you will know that you belong to God for all of time and all of eternity.

---

(1) Jeremiah 17:9, KJV. (2) Jonah 2:9, KJV. (3) Psalm 39:5, KJV. (4) Psalm 90:4, KJV. (5) 2 Peter 3:8, KJV. (6) Psalm 90:5-6. (7) Psalm 102:11-12, KJV. (8) Psalm 90:2, KJV. (9) Psalm 90:10, KJV. (10) James 4:14, KJV. (11) Ephesians 5:16, KJV. (12) John 9:4, NIV. (13) John 17:4, KJV. (14) Mark 2:5, KJV. (15) 2 Corinthians 6:2, KJV. (16) Cf. Hebrews 3:7-8. (17) 1 Kings 18:21, KJV. The Bible verse marked NIV is taken by permission from The Holy Bible, New International Version, copyright © 1973, 1978, 1984 International Bible Society, East Brunswick, New Jersey

---

7
Families Growing in God Today

"Choose for yourselves this day whom you will serve. . . . But as for me and my household, we will serve the Lord."
Joshua 24:15, NIV

A True Love Story

Dave Roever

Dave Roever, a frequent guest speaker at Billy Graham Crusades, was severely wounded in Vietnam in July, 1969. Before Roever was flown to the States, he was hospitalized in Japan. His story is an incredible account of tragedy and triumph, of horror and heroism. His suffering was intense, but the real pain was the question: "Will my wife, Brenda, have me back?" Now Brenda was coming to see him—her first visit since a phosphorus grenade exploded six inches from his right ear. Here is a story of love.—ED.

My moment of blackest despair occurred in Japan. A medic was foolish enough to grant my request for a mirror. He held it up in front of me—one of those magnifying mirrors, no less.

When I looked in that mirror, I saw a monster, not a human being, certainly not Dave Roever. My face was covered with charred black skin; it was swollen on the left side almost to the width of my shoulders. My left eye—the one I could see out of—seemed to bug out of its socket.

And the right side? It was nearly flat; a few scraps of dead flesh hung by their sinews from the bones of my skull. Liquid oozed from the flesh that was left. There were a few pouches of swelling where the flesh still had circulation, but for the most part my cheek had been blown away. It opened up down through my lower gums to my chin, way back to the muscle. I could look inside my head.

My gums were charred. My teeth were black. My tongue was

Dave Roever is president of Roever Evangelistic Association. He and his wife, Brenda, are the parents of two children. They live in Fort Worth, Texas. This article is taken from testimonies delivered at Billy Graham Crusades and from "Welcome Home, Davey," by Dave Roever and Harold Fickett, ©1986 Dave Roever, Word Books, Publisher, Waco, Texas.

still swollen, filling the mouth cavity. I had no right ear at all, and no hair, and I could see patches of exposed bone, especially above my ear at my brow. The right half of my nose was gone; I had only one nostril. My right eye lacked the eyelid—just a big gray eyeball sitting there.

I also got a glimpse of the gaping hole in my chest. I could see the bumps on my esophagus, the tendons in my throat. I could see my ribs. I could see organs moving around inside me. Everything looked wet. The three outside fingers on my right hand were almost severed. Only one finger on my right hand was still attached—my index finger was undamaged, not even burned.

When I looked in that mirror, I was struck with a lightning bolt of soul-destroying pain. My soul seemed to shrivel up, to collapse in on itself, to be sucked into a black hole of despair. I was left with an indescribable and terrifying emptiness. I was alone in the way that the souls in hell must feel alone. Jesus used the words of the psalmist when he cried, "My God, my God, why hast thou forsaken me?" (Matthew 27:46, KJV). The words registered my own feelings of desertion.

When the medic walked away, I reached over, wrapped my little finger around the tube going into me and yanked it out. I assumed it was my lifeline, filling me perhaps with the blood on which my life depended. I lay there waiting to die, wanting to die, but nothing happened except I began to feel hungry. I had pulled out the tube that was feeding me.

My thoughts and fears focused on Brenda. The first time I asked her to marry me she slapped me, saying 13 was too young. So we waited—until she was out of high school. Brenda and I didn't build our relationship in the backseat of a car; instead we built it on the front seat of church. We put Jesus first.

My final words to Brenda before I left for Vietnam with the U.S. Navy were, "Baby, I'll be back without a scar." Wearing my dress blues, I looked sharp, but she would never see me like that again.

Now I couldn't imagine that she could love me and play beauty to the beast I had become. "If I live through this," I thought, "I will be a freak. She is too young to be stuck with somebody like me. Somebody else will come along who can give her better than I can, and she'll take him."

I was flown from Japan to Randolph Air Force Base in Texas. I had been wrapped in bandages for the trip—yards and yards of bandages. From there I was transported in a convoy of ambulances to Brooke Army Medical Center at Fort Sam Houston in San Antonio. Incredible as it may sound, almost two weeks after my injury, when the doctors opened me up to do surgery in San Antonio, I burst into flames again because of the chunks of phosphorus still inside. I spent four weeks in an intensive care unit and another eight months in the burn ward for skin transplant operations.

For the first visit by relatives, only Brenda could come in. I felt tremendous anxiety, as if the tracheotomy hadn't been performed and I was suffocating once more. I waited for her to walk through the door, wondering how she would react when she saw me, wondering what the expression on her face would be, wondering if she could accept me. I felt as though my whole future, my whole identity, my life itself, depended on the look on her face when she saw me.

Just moments before Brenda arrived, a woman had come to visit her husband who was next to my bed. With no skin left on his body, he was doomed to die. She took off her wedding ring, placed it between his feet and said, "You're embarrassing. I couldn't walk down the street with you." Then she left. Fear gripped my heart as I watched the man die of a broken heart before he could die of a burned body.

How would my 19-year-old wife react to me? Then Brenda walked in. She was gorgeous. She had a hospital gown on, but I could see she had dressed up for her man.

In an instant I knew that she had remained absolutely faithful to me, that she had lived for me and kept herself chaste for me during those months of separation. The memory of her love had helped to protect me from temptations; it had kept me from violating her trust, and somehow my first feeling upon seeing her was of her worthiness, her fidelity. She was beautiful, possessed of an inner radiance which came from her relationship with God.

Brenda walked straight up to my bed, paused at the chart, read the tag on my arm and, showing not the slightest tremor of horror or shock, bent down and kissed me on what was left of my face. Then she looked me in my good eye, smiled and said, "Welcome home, Davey. I love you."

To understand what that meant to me you have to know that that was her most precious pet name for me. By calling me Davey, by invoking and embracing once more the intimacy of her knowledge of me, she said exactly what I needed to know. By using her term of endearment for me, she said, "You are my husband. You will always be my husband. You are still my man." That word of tenderness was a creative word of perfect love which cast out my fears.

All I could say was, "I want you to know I'm real sorry."

She asked, "Why are you sorry?"

"Because I always wanted to look good for you. Now I can never look good for you again."

She grinned and said, "Oh, Davey, you never were good-looking anyway." And that was the beginning of the deep psychological and spiritual healing which eventually quenched the fire of my ordeal so that I could face the world again.

Determination kept me alive, but it took love to heal the wounds.

You've given me so much—
a home where weary hearts can rest,
a family I adore,
given to me out of love,
from Your own heaven's store
and even in the midst of trial,
of painful hurts and self-denial,
I've gained a gem beyond all cost:
a spirit-growth that can't be lost
or measured in an earthly way.
And so I say,
Thank You, Lord, for these things;
because of You
my whole heart sings.
　　　—SHARON LEE ROBERTS
　　　　Waterford, Connecticut

Looking Forward to Marriage

H. Norman Wright

I don't know of any couples who marry with the specific purpose of beating one another physically, having an affair or divorcing. But these events occur in the lives of couples who profess Jesus Christ as their Lord and Savior. What can you do as you anticipate marriage? How can you prepare?

Before starting out on a long journey, a wise driver will try to determine what he is most likely to encounter along the way. How are the roads? Will there be any detours? What will the weather be? If he can know some of these things ahead of time, he will be better prepared when he gets to a place where his progress could be hampered without this foreknowledge.

Statistics prove that prospects for a successful marriage are not very encouraging. I see three reasons why marriages dissolve.

First, one or both persons fail to understand the stages and changes of individual development—the seasons of their marriage—and how these affect their marriage.

H. Norman Wright is director at Family Counseling and Enrichment in Santa Ana, California; a professor of counseling at Talbot Theological Seminary in La Mirada, California; and the author of numerous books. He and his wife, Joyce, are the parents of two children. They attend Hollywood Presbyterian Church. ©1983 H. Norman Wright.

Second, people have an inadequate basis upon which they build their personal identity and security. The best basis for marriage comes from the One who instituted marriage in the first place, but for many the teachings of God's Word have not been incorporated in depth into their lives to transform both their identity and their security.

Third, some marriages dissolve because the partners were never prepared for marriage and because their expectations about marriage were totally unrealistic. David Mace, a pioneer in the field of marriage enrichment, describes this lack of preparation: "When I try to reconstruct, in counseling with couples, their concepts of the making of a marriage, I find that it adds up to a most confused hodge-podge of starry-eyed romanticism, superstition, superficial concepts and laissez-faire. Seldom do I find any real understanding of the complexity of the task of bringing two separate individuals into delicately balanced coordination of each other's thoughts, feelings, wishes, beliefs and habit patterns."*

Young people in our society spend more time preparing to obtain their driver's license than they do preparing for marriage.

Many marriages are like the house built upon sand—they have been built upon a weak foundation of dreams. When we dream, our minds do not have to distinguish between reality and fantasy, so we are able to create without restraint. Our dreams may be starting points for successful endeavors, but dreams that are not followed by adequate planning usually do not come true.

Marriages built on dreams are risky because dreams do not consider the disappointments and changes that are inevitable in every marriage. When the seasons change and the rains of reality and the winds of stress blow upon such marriages, the relationship that should hold them together crumbles. Much more is involved in fulfilling dreams than merely expecting them to come true.

First, consider what you have to offer to another person. Too often we spend time and energy endeavoring to find the "right" person. Becoming the "right" person ourselves is more important. Entering a marriage relationship with a positive self-concept and identity built upon who God is and how he sees us is a tremendous wedding gift to our partner.

Entering marriage with a desire to give and develop intimacy is a healthy choice. Some enter marriage though as a means of gaining a reprieve from an unhappy situation.

Usually it is women who grab for a "jailbreak marriage," although men have been known to use marriage as an escape from their own parents too. Marriage under these circumstances usually carries a load of unrealistic expectations. One of the sources of marital conflict is that when people marry they often do not get what they expected to receive—and they receive what they did not expect to get.

When individuals enter their marriage from a deficit position, a strain is immediately placed upon the relationship. The spouse becomes the "answer" to unmet emotional needs, love, acceptance and happiness. The marriage partner is idealized. Faults and defects are overlooked or denied.

Second, before you enter marriage, commit yourself to having thorough premarital counseling with your minister or a counselor. If a couple or individual says, "I really don't need any counseling or preparation," watch out! I have never yet met a couple who could not benefit from the sessions of premarital preparation.

Third, think about the realities of marriage in addition to your emphasis upon the romantic. Romance is important! By preparing for the realities of the relationship, you can maintain the romantic level in your marriage. But how can a couple prepare? By careful thought and discussion of significant relationship areas.

Here are some questions and thoughts to guide you in your relationship: What expectations do you have for your marriage, and what expectations does your future spouse have? Are the expectations realistic? Can they be met? Bringing expectations into the open and examining them is necessary. In premarital counseling I ask the couples as individuals to list 25 expectations they have for their future spouses to fulfill after they are married. Then I ask them to write a short paragraph describing the effect each expectation will have on their marriage if it is not met. Each person reads his/her future spouse's list of expectations and decides which expectations are reasonable and attainable and which are not.

If I were seeing you in premarital counseling, I would ask you to bring a list of 10 specific indications as to why this is the time of your life to marry and 12 specific reasons why you want to marry the other person.

Unfortunately some people marry for the wrong reasons. Here are some unhealthy reasons for marriage. If you were to construct a list and discover that any of these reasons appear either on your list or in your own mind, you should spend time discussing them with your fiancé or your minister.

(1) To spite or to get back at your parents.

(2) Because of a negative self-image—marrying your fiancé will make you feel worthwhile and will give meaning to your life.

(3) To be a therapist or counselor to your fiancé.

(4) Fear of being left out! Fear of being left single.

(5) Fear of independence.

(6) Marrying on the rebound—you were hurt in a former love relationship and to ease your hurt you immediately choose another.

(7) Fear of hurting the other person—you are afraid of what will happen to your fiancé if you break up even though you know that marriage is not the answer.

(8) To escape an unhappy home.

(9) Because you are pregnant or your fiancée is pregnant.

(10) Because you have had sex.

Here is one way to determine if you are ready for marriage. These have been called marriageability traits! How many of these are present in your life?

(1) Adaptability and flexibility—the ability to change and adapt.

(2) Empathy—the ability to be sensitive to the needs, hurts and desires of others, to feel with them and experience the world from their perspective.

(3) The ability to work through problems.

(4) The ability to give and receive love.

(5) Emotional stability—accepting one's emotions and controlling them.

(6) Open, honest and emotional level of communication.

(7) Similarities between the couple themselves.

(8) Similar family background.

Marriage is a miniature "body life" concept where husband and wife join to grow toward maturity—through a close, vulnerable relationship—with the ultimate purpose being to honor and glorify God, letting their lives reflect the presence of Jesus Christ. Marriage is a school where we learn to be flexible, to live in harmony with each other, to walk together as one, to strengthen and complement each other as we fulfill our corporate and individual dreams, hopes and ambitions in our journey through life.

Prepare for your marriage. Be realistic and reflective.

---

*Taken by permission from "Marriage Is Relationship in Depth," by David Mace, in "Marital Therapy: Psychological, Sociological, and Moral Factors," ed. by H. L. Silverman, ©1972 Charles C. Thomas, Publisher, Springfield, Illinois

The Education of an Insensitive Father: "I Will Never Forget That Moment"

Bill Middlebrook

Winter came early and hard in 1977. A blizzard and a record number of consecutive sub-zero days added up to one of the worst winters of Ohio's history. Our older sons, who were eight and nine then, were unable to go to school for the entire month of February because of the severe cold and a scarcity of heating fuel. The boys thought it was great for the first few days but soon they became bored. Not only were they unable to go outside into the biting cold, but constantly ice-glazed windows prevented them from even being able to see outside.

My wife endured the confinement with three active kids with her typical patience. However, she was relieved one day when, because of the weather, I was unable to go to work. She grasped the opportunity to turn over the entertainment duty to me, and I willingly accepted the challenge.

After depleting my reserve of "rainy day" childhood game ideas (about 15 minutes), I suggested that the boys have an art contest.

Bill Middlebrook is an internal auditor for Washington State University in Pullman, Washington. He and his wife, Juanita, are the parents of three children and live in Pullman. They attend Church of the Nazarene in Moscow, Idaho. ©1987 Bill Middlebrook.

They weren't known for their artistic ability or even their desire for art, but they liked the idea, especially after I suggested that the objects of their artwork be each other.

They went to the kitchen table with their paper and crayons in hand and began the task. As they took turns posing, one could see a future artist in their methods. Thumbs up, noses twitching, mouths screwing, each worked diligently to create the best reproduction of his brother on paper.

At last the job was completed. I was to be the judge. Scott first revealed his picture of his brother, Tim. Tim's face was covered with freckles. At the age of nine, he had few areas of his face that were unspotted. Scott had captured this attribute well in the reproduction of his brother. Tim's freckled face stood out like the proverbial "sore thumb."

I poured out praises on Scott. "Scott, this is great!" I exclaimed. "It looks just like Tim. You really did a great job!" Scott proudly taped his masterpiece on the family art showplace, the refrigerator, and sat down.

Tim then brought his creation to the judge. I took one look and began to laugh. Tim had given Scott a BIG head, BIG eyes and BIG nose on a tiny body. It was like one of those caricature sketches mass-produced by amusement park artists. Between my bursts of laughter, I said, "Tim, this is terrible. It doesn't look anything like Scott. Are you trying to be funny?" My derogatory remarks were emitted without a speck of sensitivity and they pierced the heart of my son. The next thing I knew, Tim had picked up his picture, wadded it in his hand, walked over to the trash can and tossed it in. He stood there crying uncontrollably.

I will never forget that moment, seeing my son suffering from the inconsiderate wounds inflicted by his insensitive father. I jumped up from my chair, hurried over to Tim, grabbed him in my arms and tried to soothe his hurt. "I'm sorry, Tim. I'm so sorry. Please forgive me. I never meant to hurt you." The easily forgiving heart of a child is wonderful. As I hugged him, he hugged me tightly back, assuring me of his forgiveness, and we stood there sobbing together.

Later in the day I retrieved the crumpled piece of paper out of the trash and put it away to remind me of that emotional moment between father and son. I've thought of the incident often during the intervening years. I hope it has not remained a part of my son's childhood memories.

To me it was a lesson. How do we value the results of our efforts and those of others? Must the results always be perfect in order to be of value, or is the intent and effort to be considered?

When Samuel went to anoint the future king of Israel, he expected God to choose the one who was most visually appealing. The first of Jesse's sons to stand before Samuel must have been a striking young man. The Scripture records, "When . . . Samuel saw Eliab, [he] thought, 'Surely the Lord's anointed stands here before the Lord.' But the Lord said to Samuel, 'Do not consider his appearance or his height, for I have rejected him. The Lord does not look at the things man looks at. Man looks at the outward appearance, but the Lord looks at the heart.' "[1]

One by one the sons of Jesse presented themselves before Samuel, but each was rejected by God's great servant. When the final son had passed, Samuel asked, " 'Are these all the sons you have?' 'There is still the youngest,' Jesse answered, 'but he is tending sheep.' "[2]

To God neither the age of David nor his lowly task mattered. God saw the heart of David, a young man who, though he was to have many struggles in the future, had a heart that was totally committed to God. Years later David wrote, "May the words of my mouth and the meditation of my heart be pleasing in your sight, O Lord, my Rock and my Redeemer,"[3] and, "Search me, O God, and know my heart; test me and know my anxious thoughts. See if there is any offensive way in me, and lead me in the way everlasting."[4] David became known as a man after God's own heart.

Our value system is not God's. We compare the beautiful child to the homely waif, the successful businessman to the civil servant, the wealthy baron to the lowly peasant, the great preacher to the timid saint, commending one and ignoring or condemning the other. But God penetrates the outward appearance, the obvious success, the eloquent speech, and he sees the heart.

Tim had worked hard at his drawing. He gave it all he had. He gave it his whole heart. He had done his best in an effort to please his dad and to evoke his praise. If I could relive that moment, I would say, "A good job, son! I'm proud of you." But, of course, to return to the past to correct a wrong is impossible. Instead I must imitate my Father now and adopt his value system for the present and the future.

When I stand before my heavenly Father to present the fruit of my effort, his value system will be wonderfully demonstrated. He will not compare my fruit to that of others. He will overlook my faults and failures and see a heart that is totally committed to pleasing him. Instead of words of derision and ridicule, his words will be those of commendation and encouragement. He will say, "Well done, good and faithful servant!"[5] and I will be exhilarated by the praise of my Father.

---

(1) 1 Samuel 16:6-7, NIV. (2) 1 Samuel 16:11, NIV. (3) Psalm 19:14, NIV. (4) Psalm 139:23-24, NIV. (5) Matthew 25:23, NIV. Bible verses marked NIV are taken by permission from The Holy Bible, New International Version, copyright ©1973, 1978, 1984 International Bible Society, East Brunswick, New Jersey

Was I wakened from sleep to call upon Thee?
For my children, dear Lord, Your mercy I plead.
Wherever they are, whatever their care,
I beseech Thee, Lord, please be there.
Do they need Your rod or Your staff this night?
Or Your power to put the devil to flight?
I leave them with You, my Lord and my God,
Trusting them fully to Thy holy love.
The Spirit has lifted the darkness so deep;
Thank You for watching while I go to sleep.
   —MARY BARBARA FAECHNER
      Botha, Alberta

Late, but Not Too Late

Rita Richards

As I looked down at my mother, I knew that the last of my parental family was slipping away. Softly squeezing her thin and delicate hand, I realized I was no longer recognized. I picked up her things which had been wrapped in a brown paper parcel, and in a daze I walked to the car park where my little blue mini stood in the sun. The heat of the metal on my hand jolted my mind back into action.

A brown paper parcel! Was this what life came down to in the end? Surely there must be more—some secret of living that I had missed. "A brown paper parcel" kept ringing through my mind until I arrived home.

I was greeted with my husband's words: "Sorry, dear. Mother died soon after you left her." Bill's voice was gentle, and his arms tender as he held me.

The days melted into years. Our son married and left home, closely followed by our daughter. Bill and I were alone. We had become

Rita Richards is a homemaker who has led Bible study and prayer groups and has worked as a counselor for the Billy Graham Mission in England. She and her husband, Bill, are the parents of two grown children. They attend Upton Vale Baptist Church in Torquay, Devon, England. ©1987 Rita Richards.

workaholics. We enjoyed work and didn't realize how much of our lives were spent in it. We were comfortable with good holidays and enough money. Yet I felt something was missing.

Then came a shocking revelation. "Mum, I'm leaving my husband," our daughter told me, her voice choking. "Can I come home?"

Weeks later we recognized that our daughter's marriage had gone tragically wrong, leaving an unhealed sadness in her life and ours. I knew what it was to be utterly powerless to help. Pondering over her many words and tears, I again wondered what life was all about. Thoughts of the brown paper parcel, still unopened in the attic, drifted across my mind once more.

About this time in our lives I began to experience a dread that something would happen to Bill. This fear, and his words as they took him into hospital because of pressure on his spinal column, finally made me decide to open my mother's parcel. Trying to be cheerful, Bill said, "It's just life's rich pattern, love. Don't worry."

As Bill spoke, I knew we were both looking for a deeper meaning to life. Why hadn't we discussed this with each other? Questions filled my mind as I climbed the ladder to the attic.

The brown paper, lying so long untouched, broke easily in my hands, and soon its contents were strewn on the floor. I forced myself to look at my mother's life. First were old cuttings of a bygone age of long dresses and long hair; music and Greek exams all passed with honors; a faded photo of her husband and children; another of grandchildren; an old purse with a few pounds in it; and a King James Bible.

Other things were there, but my hand went unhesitantly to the Bible. As I picked up the Book, a verse struck me from its thin pages: "For God so loved the world, that he gave his only begotten Son, that whosoever believeth in him should not perish, but have everlasting life."[1] I read the words over and over again and then gently closed the Bible's tattered covers.

Next came the diary. Sitting alone on the floor, I opened the leather-bound book. A different handwritten Scripture text was on every page, and under the text, not a record of the day's doings, but what had been learned about life. With a lump in my throat I read under one day's heading: "Learned to hand everything over to him to use for his purpose."

Turning the pages and expecting to find condemnation of me because Mother had gone into a nursing home, I found instead, written a few days after her 88th birthday, the verse: "And they shall see his face; and his name shall be in their foreheads."[2] Under that text were her last words, "Oh, Lord, haven't I learned enough?"

Gathering up everything from the parcel and putting it back, I hurried to answer the phone. "Your husband has come around, and everything is fine. You may visit him tonight." The brisk voice of a nurse, somewhere in the labyrinth of the hospital, reached my ear. It was only then that the tears came.

Later, when we were forced to take an early retirement because of Bill's health problems, the brown paper parcel went with us. After living in our home for many years, we moved to a new area.

"We're Christians," our new neighbors told us over the garden fence. Neither Bill nor I had heard the word "Christians" for years. We joked about it, and life settled down. Bill's health improved. Slowly and kindly our neighbors' lives showed that they were indeed authentic Christians.

One Sunday morning I said, "I'm going to find out for myself, Bill." The words surprised him, and the fact that I went to church amazed us both.

After the sermon I began to think seriously about God. There seemed to be a special kind of love in the air. Was this what I had been wanting? Was this the Way?

Then this God, about whom I had begun to think, worked amazingly in Bill's life. "You don't need to ask anyone else to take you to church—I will," he said.

I couldn't believe it! Bill had been so adamant in the past. We went to church together, and that day I experienced a happiness I was quite unable to explain, even to myself. Nevertheless, as we were leaving in the car, Bill said, "I'm going only for your sake, and I don't want to hear anything about going regularly or about baptism!"

We did, however, continue to go to church each week. I soon learned that our pastor did indeed "walk with God." Everyone spoke of "sharing" and "caring," of "brothers" and "sisters." One week we were "not to strive," and the next "don't just sit there but get up and go!" It all seemed confusing, but we began to learn. Every word underlined in my mother's Bible slowly began to have meaning for me.

Finally, after one particular sermon, I had the wonderful experience of letting go of all my old selfish ideas, of asking God to forgive me and of saying with my whole heart, "Jesus is Lord."

I would make sure that our children knew that I would be with Jesus and that I too would "see his face."[2]

That Easter I stood with our son and daughter and watched Bill's baptism. That day I knew not only joy but the wonderful, tremendous patience of the Lord. He had gone before us and "hemmed" us in with Christians on both sides of our new house. He had waited and loved and cared.

I'm not lonely anymore. I have the biggest spiritual "family" worldwide.

---

(1) John 3:16, KJV. (2) Revelation 22:4, KJV

Next to inviting Christ into my life, the most important decision I ever made was about whom to marry. Once that decision was made, I knew that it was a lifetime relationship. Making that relationship a happy one has required give and take. Insisting on having one's own way invites disaster.

In our home no misunderstanding, no matter how small, is permitted to go unsettled before we sleep. Praying together and asking forgiveness of God and of each other restores love.

—A. RAY NEPTUNE

The Kidnapping

Bonnie G. Wheeler

Dusk settled over the empty parking lot as the lights in the building winked out one by one. I quietly watched as a solitary figure locked the front door and shuffled toward his car. The slump of his shoulders told a mute story of exhaustion and discouragement.

I knew my victim well, having long studied his routine. He was right on schedule. He opened the car door and dropped wearily into the front seat. Obviously tired and preoccupied, he didn't even notice me, huddled in the concealing shadows of the back seat. He fumbled lethargically with his keys, then started the car. "Don't make a move!" I gruffly ordered.

He flinched with surprise at the unexpected sound of my voice, then cautiously asked, "What's going on?"

"This is a kidnapping!" I tersely replied.

Shock slowly registered in my victim's voice, "You . . . you are

Bonnie G. Wheeler is a free-lance writer and speaker. Her articles have appeared in many Christian magazines, and she has written several books, including "Challenged Parenting" and "Of Braces and Blessings." Mrs. Wheeler and her husband, Dennis, are the parents of five children and live in Williams, California, where they attend Williams Neighborhood Church (Christian & Missionary Alliance). ©1984 Bonnie G. Wheeler.

kidding . . . aren't you?"
"Never been more serious in my life," I replied.

The past six months of my life read like a textbook case on stress and its cumulative effects. We had moved from a large metropolitan area to the country, and instead of the anticipated peace and tranquility, our lives assumed a soap-opera quality.

While our family struggled in its adjustments to a new lifestyle, the wettest winter in years helped us discover every leak in the roof of our Victorian dream home. The dream turned into a nightmare when the house flooded and the insurance company refused coverage.

One of our children had an appendicitis attack; another was involved in a bus accident; all six exchanged cold and flu like hand-me-down clothes. Then my hitherto healthy husband, Dennis, became seriously ill, and our finances quickly became another disaster as the effects of rising water and rising medical bills took their combined toll.

The doctor told Dennis to avoid stress! Then during his lengthy convalescence, I started noticing personality changes in him, and I took them all personally.

After coping with all the changes and trying to overprotect Dennis from stress, I awoke one morning with a paralyzed face. The doctor told me to avoid stress and to get a lot of rest.

One afternoon, between storms, Tim, our eldest son, and I were talking about the calamitous events that had occurred since our move. He suddenly avoided meeting my eyes as the subject of marriage came up. "You know, things sure have changed between you and Dad," he almost whispered. "All my life I've been kinda jealous of your relationship with each other. I used to feel left out. You two were so close that I almost felt like there wasn't any room for me."

"And now?" I hesitantly asked.

Tim's voice was soft—so soft that I had to strain to hear the answer I already feared: "Not anymore, Mom. Not anymore."

Both products of broken homes, my husband and I had always set a high priority on maintaining our close relationship. But now we were like two experienced ballroom dancers who, after long years of practice and anticipating every move, were out of sync and were awkwardly stepping on each other's toes. After the months of constant strain, the music of our marriage was changing from a lovely familiar old waltz to an unknown cacophony. We withdrew to separate corners of the ballroom in self-protection.

Dennis' work hours increased until there was no longer time or energy for our special dates. The jokes and laughter ended. The lines of communication on which we had once prided ourselves became tangled and unused. After 20 years of marriage we were more like strangers than partners.

During those months of stress, my once-lengthy prayers were often reduced to feeble cries of "Help!" My once-extensive Scripture reading was mostly confined to a daily Psalm.

Shortly after my talk with Tim I was reading in Psalm 84: "Happy are those who are strong in the Lord" (I wasn't feeling too strong just then), "who want above all else to follow your steps."*

That verse, added to Tim's use of past tense in describing our marriage, broke through my crusty layers of self-protective numbness. "Lord, I can't follow in Your steps and I can't just huddle in a corner, helplessly watching our marriage die, but what can I do?"

After my prayer I had the strong impression that the Lord wanted us to go away for a few days. "But, Lord! There's no time, no money. And anyway, Dennis probably will just say 'no.' " I swallowed hard. "And, Lord, I'm not sure I want to go away with this stranger—my husband."

Again there was that strong impression—Go! Reluctantly I asked Dennis about going away, and just as I had expected, he refused. "There's no time, no money," he stated.

Still that strong urge to go away persisted. I decided that if Dennis wasn't going to work with me, I would proceed on my own. With a prayer for our marriage, a deep gulp and a big step of faith, I took the last of our money, made arrangements for the children and set out in reluctant obedience. God's command was to go; the next step had been strictly my own idea.

I moved to the front seat. "You're being kidnapped," I announced to my startled victim.

"But . . . but what about the kids?" Dennis sputtered. "Church, your deadline, we can't afford . . . "

"It's all taken care of," I assured him. "And we can't afford not to," I softly added. "Now please drive!"

Dennis stiffened with shock, and I fully expected him to turn around and head toward home. Then he visibly relaxed and drove.

"Celebrating an anniversary?" asked the friendly hotel clerk.

"No," Dennis answered with a straight face. "I've just been kidnapped!"

The clerk nervously handed me the room key.

For the first time in months we really talked. Seriously, earnestly, honestly—about our marriage, where it was headed and what we wanted to do about that direction. There were apologies, tears and choked-up voices, but no arguing. When we finished talking, we prayed together with reassurance of our love and a renewed commitment to keeping that love alive. We held hands, we laughed, we had fun together for the first time in months. We had always known there was healing in tears; that weekend we learned of the healing in laughter.

Monday morning our alarm went off 30 minutes earlier than usual. It was follow-through time, and together we made a list of resolutions:

• We will talk to the doctor together (we discovered that his personality changes were a reaction to medication, not to me).

• We will sort our priorities to lessen the stress on us all.

• We will no longer ignore danger signals in our relationship.

• We will be more aware of, and sensitive to, each other's needs.

• We will work at keeping communication lines open.

• We will face and deal with issues as they come up—there will be no more retreating to separate corners.

• We will fight for our marriage.

• We will uphold each other in our walk with Jesus, realizing that he is our stabilizer in times of stress and pressure.

• We will study and pray together daily.

Morning by morning we reconnected the lines of communication that had been severed by months of constant stress. We still step on each other's toes occasionally, but there is no more retreating to the corners of the room. We just keep on working at it until we are once again back in step.

The other evening Tim caught us cheek-to-cheek in the kitchen. "Hey, you two!" he exclaimed. "I'm starting to get jealous again."

*Psalm 84:5, TLB; taken by permission from The Living Bible, copyright ©1971 Tyndale House Publishers, Inc., Wheaton, Illinois

8
Discovering God's Love Today

"This is how God showed his love among us: He sent his one and only Son into the world that we might live through him."
1 John 4:9, NIV

Racing for God

James C. Martinson,
as told to Christine Dubois

On June 29, 1968, I was a sergeant in Vietnam. I had sent my men to get resupplied from a helicopter. The helicopter was flying off when I turned around and started jogging to the top of the hill. I got about halfway up the hill when one of the men stepped on a land mine. The explosion picked me up and blew me over backward.

On July 4 I woke up in the hospital and looked at the end of my bed. Both my legs were gone—my toes were gone, my ankles were gone, my knees were gone—all was gone up to about three inches above my knees on both legs. I felt empty. I was frustrated. I was angry. And I was particularly discouraged because my dreams had been to become a downhill racer in snow skiing.

I had grown up in Sumner, Washington, played football, basket-

James C. Martinson is service manager for Puyallup Heating and Air Conditioning in Puyallup, Washington. He and his wife, Kathy, are the parents of three children and live in Puyallup, where they attend Bethany Baptist Church. Christine Dubois is a free-lance writer specializing in church communications. She edits "Olympia Churchman" and is co-editor of "Washington Christian News." She and her husband, Steven E. Bourne, live in Seattle, Washington, where they attend St. Andrews Episcopal Church. ©1984 Billy Graham Evangelistic Association.

ball and baseball in high school and ran a little bit of track. But the sport I was interested in above everything else was skiing. My dream, my desire, my goal, was to be involved with the U.S. Downhill Ski Team.

My mom's side of the family was religious—that is what I thought they were—but they did have a relationship with Jesus Christ. My grandfather was a godly man, a minister. He tried to talk with my dad, my brothers and me about Christ, but I always ran from him. When he talked Christianity to me, I would say, "Well, I've gotta go." When my brothers and I saw him coming, we would go out the back door and climb into our treehouse. We just didn't want to have anything to do with spiritual things.

After graduation from high school I enrolled in college simply because there was a draft deferment for college students. However, I dropped out of school and started skiing. So I was drafted. I didn't mind, though, because I had my life all figured out. Even the military wasn't going to mess me up with that.

While I was stationed in Hawaii for six months, I got involved in surfing and partying. The mentality of almost everybody in my barracks was that we didn't need God. We didn't need anything but a good time. As long as that good time kept coming, we didn't need anything else.

Six months later the whole bunch of us, except for one, was in Vietnam. Now there was no laughing and joking about God. The guys were serious. Is there a God? If there is a God, how can we know him? And I was one of those who was asking questions.

After my injury I was flown back to Madigan Army Medical Center in Tacoma, Washington. I spent the next nine months in the hospital and three months more as an outpatient. I was bitter toward our country. I was bitter toward people. I hated God. I hated people looking at me. I was obnoxious. I cursed anybody who looked at me in a funny manner.

I bought a new sports car—canary yellow, 350 horse—a beautiful car! I bought a new boat. I started spending every night using alcohol, drugs, marijuana. But none of that filled the emptiness in my life.

About a year and a half later I came to the point where I was going to commit suicide. I was going to take my car, go fast and hit a tree. A friend stopped me that night by taking the keys from me.

At that point three Christians came into my life and began to explain to me, each in an exciting, unique way, how Jesus Christ could change my life. One of them was Frank Mathison. We had been drafted together. He told me how he had met Jesus Christ. I replied, "I can't believe in a God who would allow me to lose my legs and our friends to be killed in Vietnam." But I watched Frank's life, and I could see that it was different. He had a peace that I didn't have.

When I met Kathy Sturgis, who would later become my wife, she told me how Christ had changed her life. I responded the same way, that I couldn't believe it. She told me that it wasn't God who caused me to lose my legs, but it was because of sin and man's rebellion that war existed in the first place. It made a lot of sense; yet I didn't want to believe it.

On November 23, 1969, another friend, Rod Fountinberry, showed me how I could invite Christ into my life. I did what he said, and the Lord changed my life. I didn't get my legs back, nor did any other fantastic experience take place, but I began to experience something new from the inside. I thought, "If God is really who he says he is, he can make me the kind of person he wants me to be." And God began to work in my life.

I started to tell people what had happened to me, and every time I would tell them, tears rolled down my cheeks. I was absolutely transformed.

Then I started working with youth. Kids have a tendency to be honest. The kids said, "We want you to begin running with us."

A good excuse was: "I can't run. I don't have legs."

They said, "You've got a wheelchair!"

So I began to train in a wheelchair. The kids ran, and I trained and got to be fairly good at it. I "ran" in some of the smaller races around the area, then got into bigger ones. As time went on, I set goals, and one of them was to "run" in the National Wheelchair Marathon, which is held simultaneously with the Boston Marathon.

I "ran" that race in 1980 and came in second. I returned in 1981 and really felt that God and I had everything together. At the beginning of the race I started out fast. I thought, "I'm feeling strong; everything is going well; I'm in the lead." The first 20 miles is mostly flat ground with some rolling hills, but then comes Heartbreak Hill. When I reached the top, I was six minutes ahead of second place. I felt great! It is a one percent downgrade from there, which is not much, but just enough that it feels good after coming up those hills.

I went into the final corner and on to the finish line where there were spectators galore—thousands were cheering. I was the first person to cross the line. I won the National Wheelchair Marathon, coming in first not only in my division but ahead of all the other runners too!

I had tears in my eyes, the hair on the back of my neck was standing up! I was excited, but I knew it wasn't just me.

I knew where I would be without Christ. What he gave me was a lot more than winning the race. It was new life that he had given me.

People usually ask me: "What changed your life? Was it wheelchair marathoning?"

I answer, "No, it was Jesus Christ."

◆ ◆ ◆

In the silent stars
    You whisper Your love to me.
Each beacon breathes "Beloved"
    in the silence of the night.

You draw close
    in all Your glory and immensity
    and stun me with the realization
    that centuries before my birth
        You put them there for me.

You knew
    that in the darkness of this night
    my heart would be despairing
and through all the ages Your candles glowed
    to remind me tonight
    You love me.
        —NANCY F. MAULDIN
        Norcross, Georgia

"We Were Empty"

Sophia R. Holloway

Something was wrong, terribly wrong, and our dream was not working out as we thought it should. On the surface things were fine, but none of us was really happy. My husband and I had ceased to care much for each other, but the marriage was there and it was all we knew. Our children, aged 15, 13, 12 and 11, were showing definite signs of rebellion and discontent.

My car, overflowing with youngsters, found its way to dancing classes, horse shows, football games, swim meets, science fairs and literary rallies. Ribbons and trophies piled up at home while our children's reputation for excellence grew. They had many natural talents, and we were able to give them the opportunity to develop these talents and to "feel good about themselves." This surely was the answer to the perplexing problems of the day. As parents of these super kids, we could feel secure in and for them. We had found the perfect scenario for the American dream! But we were not satisfied. We were an empty bunch.

I was smart enough to know that parents cannot find themselves

Sophia R. Holloway lives in Covington, Louisiana. She and her husband, Luther, are parents of four children and attend Dove Park Church of God. ©1981 Sophia R. Holloway.

in their children, so I tried to fill the empty spaces of my life with interesting pursuits. Painting followed writing and was in turn displaced by photography. A fully equipped darkroom kept me involved for a time. But the empty spaces in me would not be filled. My evening cocktail hour was starting earlier and earlier. My husband was busy with the work he loved and with worthwhile civic causes. But he too had empty spaces crying to be filled.

I had been raised in a religion, thoroughly saturated with it, but I knew that was not the answer either. I did not believe in Jesus, angels, devils or any of that. If there was a God at all, he and I were not on speaking terms. In fact, one of my goals was to protect my children from the inhibiting influence of religious fantasy, superstition and guilt. I had had enough of that to last a lifetime!

So here we were, cheerfully bouncing along on the surface, masks securely in place, but hurting and desperate on the inside. Our eldest daughter and son were already taking the first steps on that too-familiar path of drugs and alcohol. What was wrong? I did not know. They had everything going for them and yet they were miserable. I attributed my empty spaces to some missed opportunity in my past, some lack of encouragement somewhere. But where were their empty spaces coming from? We were doing our very best to see that all their potentials were being developed.

I thank God now for people in my background who prayed. I did not know God, but some of them did, and we were their long-standing prayer request. God heard those prayers, reached down and, one by one, picked us up and set us on the road of life.

God started with our eldest daughter, Betsy, aged 15. For a time she had been part of a church youth group. I thought that was harmless enough. She went to the meetings and sang in the youth choir, but away from church she went her own rebellious way. But God was plowing that field. Finally after seeing the film "Time to Run," Betsy accepted Jesus Christ as her Lord and Savior, and he took over her life.

The change in her was apparent at once, although I was unwilling to accept the reason behind the change as real. I was glad she was happy at last and seemed to have found something, but I wanted no part of it myself. I was sure I had just as much right to my agnostic way as she had to her new way of faith.

Betsy began to talk to her brothers and her sister, and God began to plow those fields too. They listened, and one by one over the course of a year they too accepted Jesus and gave themselves to him. They did not say much about it to us, their parents, and what they did say we would not hear. But the change in their lives and hearts was too evident to miss. Betsy talked to us as often as we would let her, but it was her new life which spoke the loudest.

I could have rationalized her changed behavior as the result of some new motivation perhaps, some trick of behavior modification. But the changed hearts were another story. I saw peace and joy in my children that I had never known. I saw love and concern for each other replace hostility and resentment. I saw it come from within, not as the result of any pasted-on rules, and it was happening while their quarreling parents and their homelife remained unchanged!

Finally I could deny it no longer. I did not know this Jesus whom my children knew, and I did not care anything about him. But I was desperate, and in my desperation I gave up. I put aside my stubbornness and yielded. After almost two years of resistance I merely said something like, "Well, all right, Lord, I admit I'm empty and miserable. If You are real and can do something about that, go ahead!"

And, praise God, he did! I don't begin to understand the change in me. But as he promised he would, Jesus came into my heart and somehow changed my darkness into such light as I never dreamed existed. There were no flashing lights or clanging bells. For me the change was gradual to the continual frustration of my eager little Betsy. For a year it seemed as if I just sat. But God was at work in me, undoing all the bondages and miseries I had brought on myself. He was healing me from the inside out and preparing me for growth in him.

During this period my husband surrendered his life to Jesus. We joined a church and learned that the Bible is true and real, and that God's Word to his people is as relevant today as it was in the beginning. God touched us with his Holy Spirit and suddenly our lives exploded into joy.

That was eight years ago. I have had times of great pain as I began to see my sinful self more clearly, but I have been comforted too. I have struggled to yield my will and to obey each new step God has for me. But with each tiny step of obedience has come freedom, release.

I have grown to know my God, not just to know about him, but to know him in an established relationship. He is my all in all and he will never let me go! The adventure of this walk with my Lord Jesus is beyond my capacity to explain, but it is real. God is real, his work in me is real.

All I did was yield my heart to him. By his grace alone I take each small step of obedience, and he does all the rest. He changes my heart and my life. He controls my circumstances and blesses me beyond belief. He pours his love and mercy upon me. He chastens and disciplines me as necessary for my good and his glory. He has filled my empty spaces with himself.

Our children are grown now. Betsy is a help and support to her husband, a staff member with Youth For Christ. Our eldest son will graduate from college this year and is preparing for seminary. Our younger son and daughter are active in the Campus Crusade for Christ ministries at their university.

My husband and I have discovered each other all over again, and over the past eight years we have grown together in a relationship of love and respect. He has become the "priest" in our family as God intended and has assumed his rightful responsibilities as head of this home.

In God's mercy he took six discontented, rebellious souls and by his grace saved us, filled our empty spaces and made us his own. Our God is so good!

God is a personal Being, and so must have a personal love. He cannot be satisfied with a garden or wilderness. Personal love demands personal love, and so God said, "Let us make man in our image" (Genesis 1:26, KJV). He created man that man might respond to his love. Man was made in the image of God. He came from the hand of God, but he broke away from God. However, it still stands that it was for love that God created man; and we believe that there is still something that ties man back to God. We know that the sinner is not the child of God, but the sinner is the creature of God with an intuition that relates him to God.
    —R. L. MOYER

From "John Three: Sixteen," by R. L. Moyer. ©1938 The Family Altar Book Shop, Sword of the Lord Publishers, Wheaton, Illinois

God's Plan for a Surgeon

C. Everett Koop

O ur world turned upside down when our 20-year-old son, David, died in a mountain climbing accident. David had been a delight to acknowledge as a son. When news of his death came, I can't describe the absolute desolation I felt. But 15 minutes after I heard the news I gathered my family together, put my arms around as many of them as I could, and prayed, "Heavenly Father, we know that David is Your son and that You gave him to us for a while. Now You've seen fit to take him back. We don't understand this. Please show us something that You will accomplish by putting us through this." That prayer was uncontrollable. It was God the Holy Spirit praying to God the Father through God the Son. I just happened to be the mouth.

I had been scheduled to speak at a prayer breakfast at a large

C. Everett Koop, M.D., Sc.D., is Surgeon General, United States Public Health Service. From 1948 to 1981 he was surgeon-in-chief of The Children's Hospital of Philadelphia, Pennsylvania. Dr. Koop is the author of more than 190 scientific articles and books on the subjects of surgery, pediatrics and biomedical ethics. Dr. Koop and his wife, Elizabeth, are the parents of four children (one deceased) and live in Bethesda, Maryland. Their home church is Tenth Presbyterian Church in Philadelphia. ©1985 Billy Graham Evangelistic Association.

church outside Philadelphia the Sunday after David's death. It was at the time of the first heart transplants, and I planned to give a message on the theme of the transplanted heart, basing the message on the verse in 1 Samuel 10:9, "God gave him another heart" (KJV).

After David's death the minister called to ask if I still wanted to come. I said that I did, and that Sunday morning I talked about the transplanted heart and then suddenly stopped. I said, "Now that's as far as I have prepared because something terrible happened in my life last week." Then I told them about David's death and my conviction that God was in charge and that he would work through this tragedy.

Several weeks later I discovered that a friend had recorded my message and printed it as a tract with a picture of a transplanted heart. That tract has had a tremendous ministry—more than eight million copies have been printed in several languages. People have told me, "My life was turned around by your tract on transplanted hearts." That is just one way that I feel that David accomplished more for the cause of Christ by his death than by his life. God is sovereign, he is in charge—that conviction has guided my life since I became a Christian.

I had godly parents and was raised in the church, but as a youth I never absorbed the Christian message. In college I attended chapel periodically. I prayed at night, but my prayers were along the wrong lines. I prayed for acceptance on the basis of my performance.

While I was in surgical training, I had little time for anything but work. I was on duty more than 100 hours a week. Then, at 29, I received the appointment as chief of surgery at The Children's Hospital of Philadelphia, Pennsylvania, a position I filled until I was called to Washington as Surgeon General.

From time to time my wife, Betty, and I attended a church in downtown Philadelphia on Sunday evenings. We went because this church had such good musical programs. One night our babysitter said to us, "Why don't you go a block farther and hear Dr. Barnhouse? He gives an intellectual message and I think you'll appreciate it."

The next Sunday morning my teaching rounds were over before 11:00, so I went out for a walk. I don't have any recollection about making a decision to go to church, but I seemed to be propelled to Tenth Presbyterian Church. From the balcony I listened to a dynamic preacher, Donald Grey Barnhouse, and I watched his responsive audience. That morning he talked about Christ being a priest after the order of Melchizedek. I didn't like what he was saying and I wanted to prove him wrong. I began to attend Tenth Presbyterian Church. Although I was a busy person, I consider it a miracle that during the next two years I never had an emergency that kept me from attending Sunday services.

I listened to Dr. Barnhouse and the extraordinary Bible teachers who filled his pulpit during his absence, and I felt the tremendous response of the people to the Word of God. It was one of the most exciting times of my life. The change in my life was gradual—there were no flashing lights. But I began to realize that the dynamic of the Gospel which I saw at work in the congregation applied to me. I was accepted in the beloved. I could not stand before God as a sinful being but Jesus Christ had shed his blood that I might be clothed with his righteousness. I was being conformed to the image of Christ.

Seven months after I began attending Tenth Church, my wife and I and our children were in Atlantic City, New Jersey. As I pushed our baby carriage along the boardwalk, I sensed that the Word of God that I had been listening to had become a part of me. I had received the gift of faith which enabled me to know that my sin had been nailed to the cross.

I became a man with a message, and I had to get the message out. I began to look for like-minded physicians. But I found that many physicians keep their lives in two spheres—a secular life which everyone sees and a Christian life which is private. When I began to have opportunities to work with Christian medical students, I encouraged them to combine their faith with their practice.

I came into the pro-life movement through my work with handicapped children. During my years at Children's Hospital I performed more operations on newborn children than any other surgeon in North America. People are wrong when they say that handicapped children have a quality of life that is so low that they should not live. I know how creative and innovative these children can become.

One boy, named Paul, required 37 operations to correct a birth defect. I performed 22 of those operations and was present when the others were performed. One time I asked Paul's mother, "What was the worst thing that happened in your life?"

She replied, "Having Paul born with defects that required all those operations."

Then I asked, "What was the best thing that happened in your life?"

She answered, "Having a son born with all those defects." I had
the opportunity of leading Paul's mother and father and their three
other children to Christ, and they have led some of their relatives
to the Lord. Paul's father has served as a substitute parent for boys
who don't have a father.

When Paul graduated from high school, he was valedictorian
and president of his class and he played varsity basketball. A year
ago he asked me to speak to a group at his former high school,
and when he introduced me he told about the relationship that
I had had with him and his family over the years. When he finished, there wasn't a dry eye in the house. Then he said, "Now
I'd like to introduce to you Dr. Koop, my doctor, my friend and
my manager."

Soon after I became a Christian, I became acquainted with the
Francis Schaeffer family. Then following a number of years when
we had little contact, I met Francis at York University in Toronto,
Ontario, Canada. I was giving three lectures, one on abortion, one
on infanticide and one on euthanasia. After the last lecture a student said to me, "Across the campus Francis Schaeffer is talking
about the same things. He is talking in the abstract; you have the
examples. Why don't you get together?"

We did get together, and I agreed to meet with the Schaeffer
family at the L'Abri Center in Switzerland. One evening by the
fireplace we talked about the influence of secular humanism on
people's thinking and about issues like abortion. By four o'clock
in the morning we had prepared on the backs of old envelopes
the outline for the book "Whatever Happened to the Human Race?"

Believing that men and women are created in God's image, I
cannot help but speak out against abortion. I believe that life issues
are like falling dominoes. After abortion comes infanticide and then
euthanasia of the elderly. When health officials in Nazi Germany
accepted the idea that there is such a thing as a life not worth living, that led to the destruction of retarded children, then senile
old people, then those with tuberculosis, then amputees, then gyp-
sies, then Slavs and finally the Jews.

This is a crucial time in my life. As Surgeon General I have opportunities to speak out on issues to groups of people who will
listen to what I have to say. I feel that God is in this—I am not
here of my own volition.

I am involved now in a program that will deal with violence which is reaching into every part of society. That includes child abuse, spousal abuse and abuse of the elderly.

Pornography is another concern. When pornography crosses with violence, it presents a tremendous health problem with implications for morality and the mental health of the country. A mixture of violence and pornography is available to young people on cable television and video cassettes, and what makes it worse, it is presented to the accompaniment of the rock music beat which has become so much a part of the culture of teenagers. I think that anyone raised on that fare will have extraordinary difficulty in having a normal, satisfying relationship with someone of the opposite sex.

People ask if I miss surgery. I tell them that I don't miss operating but I do miss the opportunity of counseling the families of the children who were my patients. Christians have the answer for the depression and futility that so many people feel, and I always tried to put my patients and their families in touch with God. When people asked, "Why did this happen to us?" I told them what I believed. I found that families in distress were willing to listen.

After David died, I put up in my office a picture of him in hiking clothes, standing on the mountain in New Hampshire. It was such a striking picture that almost no one would leave the office without saying, "Is that your son?"

When they asked, I would answer, "Yes. Shortly after that picture was taken, he was killed while climbing. The world called it an accident." Then I would tell them about my grief and my faith in the sovereignty of God. I said, "David was taken from us for reasons we may never know, but I can give you a long list of what we do know now. We know that this is what God has willed for us at this time." I told people in my office, "If I were not completely convinced of the sovereignty of God, I couldn't take care of your child." It was amazing what that did for people.

If I were describing my career the way I thought about things years ago, I would say that it all held together on a series of coincidences that were as thin as a cobweb. But I know now that God has been in charge. I see the unbelievable dovetailing of little things that lifted me to a position of world leadership in pediatric surgery and then to the call from the President of the United States to the position of Surgeon General. It all hangs together on the solid line of God's plan.

A Brand-New Perspective

Betsy King, as told to James R. Adair

G olf became a special part of my life when I began taking
lessons at age 10.

My parents had been athletes in college and encouraged me to
become involved in various sports. Growing up as a tomboy, I even
played tackle football with the fellows where we lived in Reading,
Pennsylvania.

In high school I played field hockey in the fall, basketball in the
winter, softball in the spring and golf during summer vacation.

In 1973 I enrolled at Furman University in Greenville, South
Carolina, having been attracted there by its nice campus, its fine
academic program and its golf course, where I could play most
of the school year. In addition to golf, I played field hockey and
basketball. But golf got the most attention. Our 1976 Furman team
won the National Collegiate Championship in the women's divi-

---

Betsy King is a professional golfer on the LPGA tour. She lives in Scottsdale,
Arizona, and attends Scottsdale Bible Church. James R. Adair is senior editor
of Victor Books, a division of Scripture Press Publications, Inc., in Wheaton,
Illinois. He has written many articles and books, including "Surgeon on Safari."
He and his wife, Virginia, are the parents of twin daughters and live in Wheaton,
where they attend Wheaton Bible Church. ©1987 Betsy King.

sion, and I finished eighth in the U.S. Women's Open, which was the best by an amateur in the previous 10 years.

After graduation in 1977, I qualified to play on the Ladies Professional Golf Association (LPGA) tour. Playing against the best women golfers in the world, I found myself tied up almost completely with my game. How well or how poorly I played affected me inwardly. If I didn't play well, I didn't feel good about myself.

But on the tour I noticed two players who seemed to be relaxed and have an inner peace that I didn't have—Donna White and Murle Breer. They were especially nice to me, a newcomer on the tour. Both were active, I learned, in the LPGA Christian Fellowship, which meets weekly for Bible study and usually attracts some 30 golfers. Through their influence I played in an FCA Pro-Am PGA tournament in Jacksonville, Florida, in 1979. Here I became better acquainted with Donna and Murle and met Margie Davis Henderson, an organizer of the tour Bible study. This led to my riding with Murle and Margie to the next tournament, and they told me about T-Off '80. It would be a conference in January at Donna White's home course, Wellington Golf Club in Florida. Here LPGA pros could come and get spiritually prepared for the long 1980 tour season. I made plans to attend the conference, the first of such events which have been held annually since 1980.

Bruce H. Wilkinson, president and executive editor of Walk Thru the Bible Ministries, spoke and his messages caught my attention. As I listened and interacted with the other women, I realized that the peace that I saw in Donna's and Murle's lives was the peace of Jesus Christ himself.

After each message Bruce gave an invitation to those who needed Christ to pray and invite him into their hearts. I had known about Christ through Sunday school and church in earlier years, but I hadn't realized that I could have a personal, day-to-day relationship with him. In one of the morning sessions I prayed the prayer that Bruce suggested. It wasn't a dramatic experience, but I sensed God's peace then and felt it afterward.

This didn't usher me into a problem-free life. To the contrary, 1980 turned out to be one of my most difficult years. I tried to put Jesus first, praying and reading the Bible every day, and weekly attending our Christian Fellowship gatherings. But this didn't seem to help my game, which was steadily deteriorating.

Some friends and family members actually believed that my spiritual activities were working against my playing well. One friend confronted me: "Betsy, now that you've become a Christian, you've lost your competitive spirit."

That fall Donna White asked me to be her partner in the Ping Team Classic in Portland, Oregon, and there I met Ed Oldfield, a teacher who has helped many golfers. He saw my problem as a mechanical one. Though I had been working hard on my game, my swing had broken down, and my shots were not on target.

That winter I moved to Arizona so that I could play regularly and keep working with Ed Oldfield. By the time the 1981 season opened, my swing was coming around, and I went on tour with my chin up.

But first I attended T-Off '81, and I learned an important principle that unlocked the dilemma I felt all during 1980: "Whatever you do, work at it with all your heart, as working for the Lord, not for men. . . . It is for the Lord Christ you are serving."*

I saw that God wants his people in different walks of life to use them wherever they are, to serve him with all their hearts. Until then I had felt guilty spending so much time working hard on my game. When I realized that I could be totally committed both to Christ and to my occupation, I felt a releasing power in me. I believed that God had given me a talent and I could give my 100 percent effort to developing it. T-Off '81 and Colossians 3:23-24 gave me a brand-new perspective to begin the 1981 tour.

As a result, I continued working hard to improve my swing, and with all my heart I began to try to bring Jesus Christ daily into everything, on and off the golf course. The 1981 season saw me gain confidence as I won my first professional tournament while playing in Japan. And on the LPGA tour I almost doubled my earnings over the previous year.

Until now the 1984 season stands out as the most memorable. It began with the Kemper Open in Hawaii, where I led the field by three strokes after the third round. Afterward I began to grow nervous thinking of my chances of finally winning my first LPGA championship. That evening I chided myself for fretting instead of praying and giving my cares over to the Lord. At that point I committed the matter to him.

The next day I played well and won the tournament by three shots. I can't say that prayer led me to victory, but it did give me perspective, making me realize that God is in control of my life.

I went on to win two more tournaments and was named the LPGA Professional of 1984, all beyond my dreams. The next year was almost as rewarding—I won two more LPGA tournaments, plus the British Women's Open. And 1986 proved to be another good year—I again won two tournaments and finished second in winnings to Pat Bradley, who had a fantastic year.

The years since I began walking with Christ have brought spiritual growth and peace. I have learned increasingly to commit each day to the Lord and live one day at a time. I see life as being like golf. Sometimes on the links I can hit good shots and not always get what I feel I deserve. Similarly, in life I often do what I feel is right but don't see an immediate reward. But as a Christian, I know that some day God will reward me for my faithfulness and obedience to him, somewhat in the way I am eventually rewarded for keeping faithfully at it in regard to my game.

I have also learned increasingly that I must keep my faith in God from day to day to let him teach me. I must trust God, and as I try to follow his instructions, though I may not fully understand, he gives me spiritual victories.

I continue to get spiritual help as, with my Bible, I meet the Lord in my devotional time, usually in the mornings. Whatever the situation, it is my intention to be living one day at a time, trying to keep Colossians 3:23-24 in mind and doing my job with all my heart unto God.

---

*Colossians 3:23-24, NIV; taken by permission from The Holy Bible, New International Version, copyright ©1973, 1978, 1984 International Bible Society, East Brunswick, New Jersey

There was a time I didn't know that God's mercy even existed. Then I heard that Jesus died on the cross and rose from the dead for our sins. Without God's mercy I would have remained a condemned soul, without hope and without provision of choice to accept or reject Jesus. It is God's mercy and compassion that gives sinful people the opportunity to receive the invitation to be forgiven and inherit eternal life.

—DENISE PETERSON

A Scientist's Search for God

Paul M. Anderson

F our friends from my church (who are also colleagues at the
university where I work) and I meet weekly for an hour to
discuss different topics of interest or concern to our everyday lives,
professions and faith. Recently we agreed to share how our faith
and professions are related. This was a significant experience. As
a result, I came to understand more clearly how important my interest and career in science has been in my embracing and experiencing the Christian faith.

I had some good experiences at church camp and Sunday school
while growing up on a farm in southern Minnesota. However, I
did not become serious about spiritual matters until after college.
During my graduate work in biochemistry at the University of Minnesota, I met Dr. Fred Smith, a professor of biochemistry. Dr. Smith
had become a Christian at a Billy Graham Crusade and was quite
evangelistic. I had many opportunities to chat with him about the
Christian faith. His concern about others and open desire to share

Paul M. Anderson is professor of biochemistry at the School of Medicine, University of Minnesota-Duluth. He and his wife, Carol, are the parents of three grown
children and live in Duluth. They attend First Lutheran Church (ELCA). ©1988
Billy Graham Evangelistic Association.

the Christian faith were impressive to me, particularly since he was an eminent biochemist in an academic science environment.

After finishing my graduate work at the University of Minnesota, I carried out research for two years as a Postdoctoral Fellow of the National Science Foundation and National Institutes of Health at Tufts School of Medicine, Department of Biochemistry, in Boston, Massachusetts, and then took a position in the Department of Chemistry and Biochemistry at Southern Illinois University, Carbondale. After four years there I went to work for Miles Laboratories, Inc. in Elkhart, Indiana.

In Elkhart my family and I joined a large church where I attended an adult Bible class on Sunday mornings. The man leading that class was a committed Christian with a message, and he took advantage of many opportunities to communicate it. We were invited to participate in a small group Bible study fellowship at their home each week. I am glad we attended, because the result was an understanding and experiencing of purpose and meaning in my life through Jesus Christ.

At that point my life could probably be considered successful by some standards (wonderful wife and family, a new home, a successful career). I loved and enjoyed science and felt fortunate to have a career in this field. Yet something was missing. What was missing was purpose and meaning in my life, and this was intensified by the tremendous beauty, order and design evident in the world as I observed it as a scientist. I was sure that there was a Creator, a Supreme Being. There had to be some purpose behind this design of things and our existence, and I was looking for that purpose.

Within my experiences with Christianity, my biggest problem had been Jesus Christ. I intellectually accepted the idea of God, but I could not accept Jesus Christ. I had many discussions and friendly arguments about him, but as I realized later, I had neglected to follow an important principle of open scientific investigation, which is to consider all the data and information about a subject before drawing conclusions. Although I had some knowledge about the Bible, I had never really read it!

During this time of searching for purpose I was influenced by two books. One was titled "The Greatest Thing in the World," by Henry Drummond (an evangelical scientist who wrote and lectured extensively on the contribution of science to Christianity). One night as I was reading it, I came across a passage that had an impact on me: "Willpower does not change men. Time does not change men. Christ does."[1] I remember that I said to my wife, "Hey, that's it!"

Another book that influenced me was "Surprised by Joy," by C. S. Lewis, in which he describes moving from theism to Christianity. He had been struggling with these issues and recalls in his book that one day he took a bus and when he came home on the bus that night, he comprehended that Jesus Christ was the Son of God. He didn't know how it happened.

That's the way it was for me. Suddenly I understood. Before I had seen Jesus Christ only as a man. Now I understood that Jesus Christ is the "visible expression of the invisible God"[2] who came to earth to live, but was put to death on the cross as a sacrifice that we may be saved from our sins. (I had not even understood that I needed forgiveness!) This was amazing! Man, created by God in his image but separated from God because of sin, cannot be reconciled with God by his own efforts because of these sins. So God himself provided a solution. The Creator of the universe took it upon himself to come and live as a man. He was wrongly understood and accused; yet willingly he went to the cross to provide a way for man to be reconciled to himself for all those who believe. Not only that, but the life and teachings of Christ give us a glimpse of how God intended that life can and should be lived.

At that time I bought a Phillips translation of the New Testament and read the entire book in about three weeks. I remember reading passages such as, "The preaching of the cross is, I know, nonsense to those who are involved in this dying world, but to us who are being saved from that death it is nothing less than the power of God,"[3] and thinking, "I understand that." Since that time I have had a sense of purpose and meaning in my life and work, and I have come to understand clearly my need for forgiveness, which I am assured of through the life, death and resurrection of Christ. I am impressed by the overwhelming experience of knowing that what little understanding I do have of these matters is also a gift of God.

After one year in Elkhart, I accepted a position as professor of biochemistry at the University of Minnesota-Duluth School of Medicine. During our first four or five years in Duluth, I learned a great deal about the Christian faith because of my involvement with the Inter-Varsity Christian Fellowship group on campus, with which I had the privilege of serving as faculty adviser. Hosting a weekly Bible study group in our home for medical students and friends for the past 13 years has been another marvelous experience. Teaching Sunday school and being involved in evangelism and other outreach efforts in our church have provided great learning experiences and opportunities for sharing my faith.

It is exciting to be involved in situations where I have opportunity to be of help when others are searching for answers, as I was, and to see others experience salvation through Christ. But while there is great joy in that, I am again impressed by the knowledge that I clearly have nothing to do with it. We do not transform ourselves or others—we are transformed by Jesus Christ.

So, how are faith and a profession in science related for me? I believe that being a Christian places added importance on being good at my work. The witness of Dr. Fred Smith was particularly significant for me because I also recognized the high quality of his work and the importance he placed on excellence. And I have a responsibility (and desire) to conduct my life in a way that is pleasing to God—that is how the world will know who God is. That is not easy most of the time, and I am thankful for God's promise of forgiveness.

An exciting area in science today is the work being done to develop a unifying theory of the fundamental nature of matter. Astronomers are looking at events at the edge of the universe. Physicists are studying the structure of the subatomic particles of matter. Both are asking fundamental questions about the origin of the universe and exciting theories are being tested.

Ultimately, questions such as "Why?" "How did it all begin?" and "What happened before that?" become important, and some theoretical physicists have attempted to deal with these issues as well. A few have proposed interesting philosophies in attempts to reconcile our modern understanding of the origin of the universe with man's destiny and reason for existence. I believe that scientific investigation such as this is legitimate and helpful for man's search for truth and understanding.

These kinds of considerations and the evidence of God's handiwork all around us are what propelled me in the direction of the Christian faith and now continue to strengthen my faith. However, I find my ultimate fulfillment in understanding God's plan as revealed through Jesus Christ. "For it is in him, and in him alone, that men will find all the treasures of wisdom and knowledge."[4]

(1) From "The Greatest Thing in the World," by Henry Drummond, The Peter Pauper Press, Mount Vernon, New York. (2) Colossians 1:15, Phillips. (3) 1 Corinthians 1:18, Phillips. (4) Colossians 2:3, Phillips. Bible verses marked Phillips are taken by permission from "The New Testament in Modern English," Revised Edition, translated by J. B. Phillips, ©J. B. Phillips 1958, 1960, 1972, Macmillan Publishing Company, Inc., New York, New York; Wm. Collins Sons & Co. Ltd., London, England

◆ ◆ ◆

We celebrate and live.
Friends gathered to be friends
   in growth
     and new direction
       and our partnership in ministry,
Finding our center
In a moment of rejoicing.

And always Your Kingdom breaks through,
Dancing like a million stars
Above our heads.

And laughter,
Like the sun of warm embraces,
Casts a glow.
   We are whole!
   We are one!
   —TERRI FISHER
    North Hollywood, California

Drug Runner

Glenn Makay, as told to Twila Knaack

I was tense as the South American Indians loaded our plane with what they called "the good bush." A light spring rain was hitting the rough dirt runway. Then, as the staccato of distant machine gun fire broke the still, night air, Rick, my co-pilot on his first illegal venture with me, looked to me for an explanation. I shrugged my shoulders and mumbled, "Who knows? Maybe some unsuspecting drug runner just collected his pay."

Quietly and quickly the laborers, with submachine guns strapped to their backs, ran back and forth along the airplane fueling it from hand-pumped, old, rusty 55-gallon drums.

As the activity of the Indians stopped, Rick and I, both drenched from rain and perspiration, strapped ourselves into the cockpit, readying ourselves for the seven-and-one-half-hour flight to a Florida landing strip. My heart pounded as I gingerly nursed the heavily

Glenn Makay (a pseudonym) and his wife live in the eastern part of the United States. Twila Knaack was administrative assistant to the president of World Wide Pictures in Burbank, California, and is the author of numerous magazine articles and several books, including "Special Friends" and "I Touched a Sparrow." She lives in Sylmar and attends Grace Community Church in Panorama City. ©1984 Twila Knaack.

overloaded plane past the flashing kerosene lamps dotting the airstrip. The plane raised into the air and flew over the Andes Mountains. It was April 10, 1978.

It wasn't just the money I knew would be waiting for me when I delivered my contraband cargo; it was the challenge of succeeding that enticed me to risk my life on these illegal drug runs. It was far from the lifestyle my minister-father wished for me.

The eldest of four boys, I grew up in western New York State where Dad was a pastor. Whenever the doors of that little country church were open—three or four times a week—I was there. I believed in God and believed the Bible because I had no reason not to. It had been planted in my life, but I hadn't taken it to heart. I had never taken the time to find out who Jesus Christ was.

After high school graduation my quest for adventure lured me into doing investigative work for a bank. That prompted me to earn my private detective's license and open my own agency. At the same time I became engrossed in flying.

When I grew restless working as a flight instructor and a pilot for various companies, I entertained crowds as a stunt pilot at air shows. On the weekends I used my musical talent to play in piano bars. In January, 1978, I moved to Florida and flew charters to islands off the coast.

My relationship with my parents was strained, and I knew they, along with their many Christian friends, were continually praying for me. I now recognize that the close calls I encountered while flying were a way for God to get my attention.

God's voice crescendoed when, in the blackness of that April night, I was jolted from my reminiscing as our plane's engines sputtered. "Fuel problems," I muttered. Without warning, both engines died, and we plunged through the utter darkness to the country beneath—Cuba. We crashed into a tree. The wings and tail disintegrated, and what was left of the aircraft spun around and bumped on the ground. I was knocked unconscious. Slapping my face, Rick revived me and yelled, "Quick, jump out the back!" Fearing an explosion, I moved fast.

Aching from bruises and bleeding from lacerations, I ran across the highway where we hid in the bushes. We had only the slightest hope of not being found.

The Cuban police arrived shortly. Their dogs immediately sniffed us out of the bushes, and in the dim glow of the moonlight we saw the machine guns aimed at us. Still in shock, I said to Rick,

"You wanted adventure. I think we're about to get some!"

We were driven in separate cars to a prison. There we were given strip searches and were interrogated throughout the night. In faltering English the political police stated that we had been arrested as counterrevolutionaries. "Do you know you could be executed for this?" they asked.

Placed in a solitary cell, I quietly began praying, "God, please forgive me for the way I've lived." I made a commitment there to Jesus Christ that whatever was ahead, I would accept it as his will and would do it.

Assurance of his presence was with me as the days stretched into weeks. When I was moved to another building in the prison complex, another prisoner, a compassionate man, asked me, "Is there anything I can do for you?"

"Could you get me a Bible?" I asked.

"Sure," he replied. "I have one I read every morning, but I'll see that you get it in the afternoons."

Although he had already been imprisoned for 10 years, he continued to live the life of a relevant Christian, retaining an exuberance and zest for living in the midst of an earthly hell. Within three months, through one of the embassies, this Christian brother helped me obtain my own paperback New Testament.

As I read it, I identified with the Apostle Paul, who wrote from his prison cell: "For I am convinced that neither death, nor life, nor angels, nor principalities, nor things present, nor things to come, nor powers, nor height, nor depth, nor any other created thing, shall be able to separate us from the love of God, which is in Christ Jesus our Lord."* These verses verified for me that through my personal relationship with Christ, I could have love, joy and peace regardless of my circumstances.

In my dungeon with its unprotected light bulb hanging from the ceiling I spent between 3,000 and 4,000 hours reading my Bible and getting to know my Savior during the many long months. One of the things that became apparent to me was the value and necessity of hearing what the Lord had to say each day as I read his Word.

During those perilous days when I never knew whether I would be alive from one day to the next, I learned to put my confidence and trust in the Lord. I received strength from the Holy Spirit who gave me peace of mind to endure.

As I read the letters Paul wrote from prison, I realized it was because of his tribulations and persecutions that he was strong.

I could associate myself with that type of attitude. Things my parents had said to me in the past came back to me.

Four weeks after arriving in prison, I was given a trial. Several of the seven judges questioned me through an interpreter while others slept through the session. An obviously predetermined sentence was given to me—eight years in Combinado del Este Prison just outside Havana.

With two cellmates I shared a 5' x 8' cubicle that had a three-tiered bunk bed. A pipe came out of the wall for a shower. Within a 20-minute period each day we could take a shower—if we didn't mind the ice cold water. The toilet was a hole in the floor. Once a week we were given soap and a blade so that we could shave. Hunger pains gripped me each morning, but all I woke up to was a cup of processed milk and a small piece of hard bread.

The evening meal sometimes included fish, which I later learned was seven years old, having come in boxes dated 1971. Most often my main meal was unprocessed rice. Several times I broke my teeth biting into the rocks in the rice.

I continued to study God's Word every day. I learned that he created us to praise him. It takes effort to do that, but it can be done whether we're locked in a cell or surrounded with good things.

After two-and-one-half years of wearing a black uniform, I, along with 32 other American prisoners, was given civilian clothes and taken to the airport. Fidel Castro had agreed to release us.

October 28, 1980, was homecoming day. Reporters and cameramen, as well as anxious, relieved relatives, were on hand at Tamiami, the small Miami airport, to greet us that afternoon.

As I descended the steps of the plane, I saw my mother and father whose hearts I had so often broken. Through letters I had told them that God, by his loving mercy, had changed my life and given me a new direction.

Today I am back in the resort area of western New York, where I grew up. My wife and I are both active in a local, dynamic community church and praise the Lord daily for the many blessings that some people take for granted.

---

*Romans 8:38-39, NASB. The Bible verse marked NASB is taken by permission from the New American Standard Bible, ©1960, 1962, 1963, 1968, 1971, 1972, 1973, 1975, 1977 The Lockman Foundation, La Habra, California

9
Ministering for God Today

"We loved you so much that we were delighted to share with you not only the gospel of God but our lives as well."
1 Thessalonians 2:8, NIV

Love in the Rain

Roger C. Palms

Friday night great thunderclouds rolled in a little while before the Crusade service was to begin. Many elderly and handicapped people were already seated in a special section on the field. They had arrived early to avoid the press of the crowds; now they were about to be caught by the storm. Then the storm broke with blinding sheets of rain and hail.

In the stands were 2,500 soldiers from Fort Jackson and other installations. They were equipped, they had rain ponchos. They could have stayed put. But out of the stands some of the troops came running, pulling off their ponchos as they came. Quickly wrapping the elderly and the handicapped in their ponchos, they assisted or carried people to shelter under the stands. Those whose wheelchairs were carried in had a place to sit; others didn't. Then a young GI called out, "These people can't stand here this long. We have to get chairs for them." So, out they went again, minus raingear, into the torrents to find chairs for the people. There was no drill sergeant telling them to do it, they did it on their own. Young kids, raw recruits, caring about others and showing love in action.

Later, though the rain let up momentarily, the service was shortened by rolling thunderheads moving back in. Mr. Graham presented God's clear plan of salvation in fewer than six minutes and gave the invitation to receive Christ as personal Savior and Lord. Hundreds came, to be counseled in the rain. One was an 83-year-old woman who refused her son's plea that she go for shelter. "No," she said. "I want to go out on that field and receive Christ." And with the rain falling on her, she did.

Many of the same troops who had helped people before were on the field again, this time with heads bowed, caps off, giving their hearts and their lives to Jesus Christ. The choir was singing, the wind was building, clouds were churning, lightning was flashing and people everywhere were streaming out of the stands to come to Christ. It was a wet night, a miracle night, a night of redemption, a night of love.

It was a beautiful night.

We are not sent primarily to be missionaries, pastors, teachers or any other kind of worker. It isn't the office I hold that signifies my service, but the way in which my heavenly Father is glorified in the common things of my life. There are little "nobodies" scattered around the world, whose lives radiate and glorify God, whose daily doings bring joy to the angels of heaven—and yet in the eyes of this world they are still nobodies.
    —JOHN E. HUNTER

From "Knowing God's Secrets: The Secret of the Effective Christian Life," by John E. Hunter, ©1965 Zondervan Publishing House, Grand Rapids, Michigan

Encouragement

Gary R. Collins

The plane was late when it landed in Omaha, and I was in a hurry. I had come to give a speech on how we can be people-helpers, and I wanted to get off the aircraft and into a taxicab as quickly as possible.

When I pushed into the aisle and moved toward the front of the plane, I hardly noticed the elderly lady who was struggling to reach the rack where her overnight bag had been placed. "Somebody should help her," I thought in passing, but I kept going—into the terminal and toward the baggage claim area.

Then it struck me! Clenched in my hand was a briefcase holding my notes about how we should help people. In my pocket was a Bible which tells me to encourage others and to give them a hand with their burdens—but I had been too rushed and preoccupied to help a fellow passenger reach some luggage. I wanted to run back to the plane, but I knew that it was already too late. Maybe some other person had lifted the suitcase down, or perhaps the

Gary R. Collins, professor of psychology and counseling at Trinity Evangelical Divinity School, has written or edited nearly 30 books. He and his wife, Julie, are the parents of two children and live in Deerfield, Illinois. ©1981 Gary R. Collins.

woman had climbed up on the seat so she could reach her possessions.

I remembered this recently when I was reading the book of Acts. Those early Christians were never too busy to help others, and apparently some of them also liked to encourage one another.

Consider Barnabas, for example; he must have been an unusual man.

He is not so well known as Abraham, Moses, Peter, Paul and the other Bible heroes. Probably nobody ever thought of him as an impressive statesman, a mighty warrior or an eloquent speaker. There is no indication that he was rich, or powerful, or famous.

But Barnabas cared about people.

His parents had named him Joseph, but the apostles in the early Church started calling him by a name which meant "consolation" or "encouragement." Barnabas cared so much about others that the meaning of his name was inserted right into the Bible. He was named "Son of Encouragement."[1]

More than once the New Testament instructs us to encourage one another, [2] but how quickly this can be forgotten when we are pressured by personal problems or intensely involved in a variety of activities. We seem to be so concerned about ourselves or so caught up in our busy schedules—as I was on that airplane—that we become insensitive to others. We forget that encouragement is not just suggested in the Scriptures; it is commanded by God.

Encouragement is difficult to put into practice. According to the dictionary, encouragement involves inspiring other people with courage and confidence. The encourager stimulates others by giving approval and assistance—but how can that be put into daily practice?

We can encourage others with words. I once had a student who purchased some 3"x5" cards and had these words printed at the top: "Encourage one another and build one another up."[3] Every week this student wrote a little note of encouragement on a card and sent it to one of his friends. Soon many of his fellow students were doing the same thing. It hardly took any time to write the notes, but they gave a tremendous lift to the people who received them and to those who wrote and sent them.

Notes of encouragement don't have to be detailed. Even a few sentences written to express your appreciation will be received with gratitude, and often with surprise, by people in your home, your church or your place of work. Have you ever thought of writing a note of appreciation and encouragement to your pastor, your boss, your spouse, a respected stranger, or even to people whom you take for granted, like the mailman, the church organist or the person who cleans your office at the end of the day?

Remember too that we can encourage people verbally. I get the impression sometimes that policemen, teachers, the people who work in check-out lines at the grocery store, airline employees, secretaries and sometimes even members of our own families hear complaints and criticism more often than they hear words of appreciation and encouragement. That can be changed immediately, starting with you and me.

In doing this we are likely to get involved in a second practical way of giving encouragement. **We can encourage others with our prayers.** Have you ever talked to someone whose needs and problems are so great that you can't think of any way to help except to pray? If we believe in the power of prayer, we have to conclude that this is the most effective way to give encouragement. By asking our loving and all-powerful heavenly Father to work in the lives of other people, we can provide encouragement which is far beyond our ability to give.

We can encourage others by expressing our confidence in them. When Saul was converted on the road to Damascus, the early Church members didn't jump up and down with enthusiasm. Saul had been the chief persecuter of believers, and it is likely that the early Christians were at first skeptical about the validity of his conversion. Some may even have wondered if Saul was planning to trick the Christians by pretending to be a convert.

When Paul arrived at Jerusalem, "he tried to meet with the believers, but they were all afraid of him. They thought he was faking! Then Barnabas brought him to the apostles and told them how Paul had seen the Lord on the way to Damascus, what the Lord had said to him, and all about his powerful preaching in the name of Jesus. Then they accepted him, and after that he was constantly with the believers."[4]

Can you imagine how Paul must have been encouraged by the confidence in him that Barnabas showed? Barnabas took a risk. What if Paul had turned out to be a deceiver after all? It was a risk which Barnabas took courageously—and Paul was encouraged.

Have you ever passed an exam, obtained a job or reached a goal because somebody else believed you could do it? We are encouraged when others show confidence in us, and by showing confidence in other people, we encourage them as well.

We can encourage others by helping and by not hindering. After Saul was accepted in the Church (and his name was changed to Paul), he and Barnabas were selected to be the world's first Christian missionaries. Off they went to places like Phoenicia, Cyprus and Antioch, helping each other and preaching about the Lord Jesus. Barnabas had been a Christian for the longer period of time, but by the end of the journey it appears that Paul was leading the missionary team and Barnabas was in second place.

In our success-dominated society it isn't easy to take second place while somebody else gets the acclaim and the attention. But not Barnabas! It was a mark of his spiritual maturity that he resisted when people tried to make him a god, submitted to the Spirit's leading, served faithfully and let God decide who was to be more prominent. Paul never had to worry about an overly ambitious co-worker. Barnabas was always willing to help, and his presence next to Paul points to another guideline for encouragement.

We can encourage others by our presence. Several years ago a family lost their teen-aged son in a car accident. When a friend came to offer his condolences, the grief-stricken parents were too distraught to welcome their visitor, so they asked him to leave.

The man went out to his car and sat there. Hours passed, and that evening a grieving family member looked out the window and noticed that the friend was still in front of the house.

"Many kind people visited us and sent flowers," one of the parents commented later, "but in our time of sorrow, nobody encouraged us so much as the man who supported us by his presence."

We can encourage others by our giving. Jesus once said that "it is more blessed to give than to receive."[5] Such giving encourages both the giver and the one who gets the gift.

The book of Acts tells about a great famine that occurred. Many of the believers were in need, and without hesitation the more affluent believers took an offering and sent the money to the needy. It was Barnabas, along with Saul, who carried the contributions to the people who were hungry.

Barnabas can be our example. He once was described as a man characterized by a gracious personality, a generous disposition, a keen desire to spot potentialities in others and a freedom from petty narrowness or self-centered ambition. The Bible states that Barnabas was a good man, filled with the Holy Spirit and with faith, and inclined to encourage others.[6]

I wish I had thought about this before that airplane trip to Omaha several years ago. I didn't do anything to help that woman with her luggage. I have changed since then. I really want to be a man who helps and encourages others. God expects it and I have discovered that it makes life more fulfilling.

Perhaps I should tell you one more thing. Whenever I go on an airplane, I look for opportunities to help my fellow passengers with their luggage! That encourages them and me!

---

(1) Acts 4:36, RSV. (2) 1 Thessalonians 5:11; Hebrews 3:13; 10:25. (3) 1 Thessalonians 5:11, RSV. (4) Acts 9:26-28, TLB. (5) Acts 20:35, KJV. (6) Acts 11:23-24. The Bible verse marked TLB is taken by permission from The Living Bible, copyright ©1971 Tyndale House Publishers, Wheaton, Illinois

◆ ◆ ◆

Please give us child-wise faith
to place our feet of clay
inside our Master's sandals—
that we can glide over tide-ripped seas,
scale ice-glazed cliffs
and dance through trials of flame,
transforming this world with God's love.
Increase our strength, enlarge our steps,
until every mile we march converges
into a one-way celebration
straight to heaven.
        —VIVIAN R. STEWART
         Oklahoma City, Oklahoma

The Vision for Making Disciples

Robert E. Coleman

The command to reach the world for Christ resounds through the Gospels. Jesus commands his followers to go and disciple all peoples everywhere, baptizing believers and teaching them to do his will.

Traditionally we have interpreted this to mean a call to overseas missionary service. Certainly this is a priority concern. More people are needed in the mission fields of the world, especially in crossing cultural boundaries with the Gospel. The number of men and women moving into this challenging ministry could well increase a hundredfold.

But is going to a distant land to work for Christ the only way to fulfill the command? A closer look at the commission in the Gospel of Matthew answers the question. "Go," "baptize" and "teach" all derive their force from "makes disciples."[1] The com-

Robert E. Coleman, Ph.D., is director of School of World Mission and Evangelism at Trinity Evangelical Divinity School in Deerfield, Illinois. He was formerly McCreless professor of evangelism at Asbury Theological Seminary in Wilmore, Kentucky. Dr. Coleman and his wife, Marietta, are the parents of three children. They live in Deerfield and attend North Northfield United Methodist Church in Northfield. ©1985 Robert E. Coleman.

mand is not to see how far one can travel in ministry, though the word "go" does stand in a coordinate relationship to the verb, emphasizing the necessity for taking initiative in contacting people. Similarly, we baptize and teach in the process of reaching the world. But it is discipling which gives validity to the other activities.

The word "disciple" translates "learner." So a disciple of Christ is one who learns of him. Assuredly as one grows in the knowledge and grace of our Lord, there will be development in his character as well as maturation in his ministry. Disciples inevitably become disciplers, reproducing again the cycle of growth.

To understand what this means we must look at Jesus and observe his way of life. As we do, we are made aware of a completely different value system. Renouncing his own rights in order to identify with our needs, he took the form of a servant, bearing our sorrows, carrying our grief and, finally, dying for our sin. As Jesus hung on the cross, people mocked him, saying, "He came to save others, but look at him! He can't even save himself!"[2] The irony is that in their derision the crowd said the truth. Of course Jesus could not save himself. That was the point. He had not come to save himself. He came to save us. He came to seek and to save the lost. He came not to be served but to serve, and to give his life a ransom for the world.[3]

On his pilgrimage to Calvary Jesus went about doing good, responding with compassion to the cry of the multitudes. Most people were appreciative, but blinded by materialism and self-centeredness they had a superficial understanding of his message. Unless spiritual leadership could be raised up to multiply the ministry of Christ, there was no way the waiting harvest could be realized.

So while manifesting God's love and power to the people, Jesus cultivated those who someday would lead them. They were called to follow him. As their number grew, he chose 12 to be with him. Peter, James and John had an even closer relationship, underscoring the principle that the smaller the group being taught, the greater the opportunity for learning.

Seldom were these men separated from him. For the better part of three years they lived and worked side by side. It was like a family, learning and growing together. In this close association the disciples were able to see the demonstration of Christ's teaching and to feel his burden for the people. Before long they were sent out to do much the same things Jesus had been doing: preaching, teaching, healing and, above all, making disciples. Though progress was painfully slow, especially in comprehending the meaning of the cross, Jesus patiently kept them moving toward his goal.

That vision was the ultimate evangelization of the world and the establishment of his eternal Kingdom. By following his plan of discipling and appropriating the power of the Holy Spirit, his objective would be fulfilled.

Our Lord had given us a model that every believer can follow. Too easily we have relegated his ministry to those persons who fit rather well-defined stereotypes of church work, such as the Sunday school teacher or preacher. Sometimes it is even more narrowly limited to trained personnel who are properly ordained or commissioned for service. However, most people cannot identify with these professional roles of ministry. For them the priesthood of all believers remains an elusive ideal. They may regard themselves as priests before God on the vertical level of prayer, but there is little, if any, comprehension of their priesthood on the horizontal plane of human relationships. This is because ministry has been equated with official church vocational callings, and not with the more undergirding servant role of discipler.

The Great Commission comes as a corrective to this popular misconception. In its focus upon lifestyle, our Lord's basic ministry becomes a meaningful option to every child of God. The homemaker, the farmer and the automobile mechanic in their natural spheres of influence have as much occasion to follow Christ's example as does the evangelist or missionary. Some persons will have special roles for which they are gifted, and their discipling will take place through that calling, whether at home or abroad. But the Great Commission itself is not a special gift or calling; it is an intentional daily servant pattern of living by which learners are led in the way of Christ.

The responsibility to evangelize the world rests upon every Christian. No one can be excused on the basis of not being called. For Jesus had made it quite clear that his discipling ministry is woven into the fabric of Christian life, and its ultimate objective, through the power of the Holy Spirit, is to bring God's Good News to every person.

The following deductions from Christ's example may suggest some practical guidelines:

1. Pray that the Lord will raise up laborers for his harvest—persons with the Shepherd's heart, who will learn his way and

be willing to lay down their lives for the sheep.

2. Take the servant's mantle. It finds expression in the compassionate response we make to the needs of people, whether physical, social or spiritual.

3. Be alert to those eager to learn of Christ. This yearning has been placed in the heart by God. A few such budding disciples are within the sphere of everyone's influence, beginning at home, and the environs where we live and work.

4. Get together with learners as much as possible. The more natural the association the better, like having dinner or playing ball together. Arrange some times for extended fellowship.

5. Accept a basic discipline to encourage obedience. That which is agreed on will depend upon the situation. It might be daily devotions, Bible study, Scripture memory, fasting or another form of abstinence, church work, personal witnessing or social action. Whatever it is, keep it relevant and growing.

6. Show how to minister. The emphasis is upon demonstration. People will catch on to our schedule of priorities, burdens of prayer and practice of witness in the context of living.

7. Involve each person in service according to his or her gifts. It is on-the-job training all the way. There is something everyone can do. As faith and skills grow, participation can be enlarged.

8. Keep them on course through continual supervision. Teach faithfulness in completing assignments. Always build self-esteem by personal affirmation and commendation.

9. Expect disciples to reproduce your vision for the Kingdom. As the process repeats itself in other disciples, and they in turn do the same, your witness will continue to reach out in an ever-expanding sphere to the ends of the earth and to the end of time.

10. Let the Holy Spirit have his way. Here finally is the secret of the Great Commission. God's work can never be done in the energy of the flesh. As this is learned, the life of Jesus becomes real; he lives and works through his disciples, and we experience the overwhelming reality of the promise: "Lo, I am with you always, to the close of the age."[4]

---

(1) Matthew 28:19-20, RSV. (2) Cf. Matthew 27:42. (3) Matthew 20:28. (4) Matthew 28:20, RSV

Then Things Began to Change

Joanne Shetler

W hen I was 12 years old, I heard Bible verses like, "Go into all the world, and preach the gospel."[1] . . . "Make disciples . . . teach people."[2] I thought, "I have to obey God. I wonder what I've gotten myself into by becoming a Christian." Still, it had made such good sense.

So with solid 12-year-old logic, I decided I should be a missionary. How could I enjoy my salvation and not share it with others?

Yet I felt so inadequate. I remember thinking, "I don't know how!" But God wouldn't accept my excuses. Of course I was inadequate. God delights in inadequate people.

At the same time I was afraid. During high school I remember wondering what missionaries did. How did they know when they were finished with their jobs? An even worse fear was of the awesome responsibility. What if all a person ever knew about God

Joanne Shetler is a translator and a consultant with Wycliffe Bible Translators in Huntington Beach, California. Currently on furlough from her work in the Philippines, she resides in Morro Bay, California, and attends First Baptist (BGC) in Paso Robles. This testimony, given at the International Conference for Itinerant Evangelists, July 12-21, 1986, Amsterdam, The Netherlands, is included in "The Calling of an Evangelist," edited by J. D. Douglas, ©1987 World Wide Publications, Minneapolis, Minnesota.

was what I told him? What I could teach wouldn't be enough.

So I did what seemed logical if I planned to be a missionary—I went to college. I graduated, but still could not understand what missionaries did. I had a file drawer full of information from mission boards, but I had nothing to zero in on.

Hoping to find a clearer direction, I took a one-year nursing course—that seemed like another logical step in case I ended up in a remote area as a missionary. Besides, it was a good way to stall for time.

I was graduated from a school of missionary medicine, but again I didn't know what to do next. I heard about a summer course which would teach me how to learn a foreign language. It seemed like another reasonable, logical move.

"Is this really how God leads people?" I wondered. Having a special dream or hearing a voice would have been much easier. But all I felt was a need, and I reasoned how best to meet that need.

Halfway through the linguistics course the pieces began to fall into place. It was during the course that I heard about Bible translation. This was a definable job, something I could do—translate Scripture for people. It was not only definable, but I would also know when I was finished. And my fear of being a hindrance to someone's knowledge about God dissolved when I realized that I could give people God's Word in their own language, for God himself could speak to them just as he had spoken to me through his Word.

It was as if God had rung bells and flashed lights. Suddenly it wasn't just logic by which I had made my decisions!

There are about 3,000 languages in the world which don't have a written translation of Scripture. One of these languages was Balangao. The people who speak this language were once headhunters and live in the mountains of the northern Philippines.

In 1962 Anne Fetzer and I were assigned to live with them to learn how they think, to see life through their eyes, to learn their language and eventually to give them God's Word in their own language.

To get to Balangao we rode a bus for three days, climbed rugged mountains for two more days and finally arrived. We were exhausted, rain-soaked, muddy and bleeding from leech bites. The people had never seen white women before and were shocked.

Balangao was only five days north of Manila, but it was centuries back from the modern world. The people were amazing. They had carved rice terraces from the sides of the mountains, and all they had to eat was what they grew.

The man who agreed to have foreigners come was upset when he saw us. "Not women!" he cried. "Don't you know it's not safe for women to be here? You need someone to take care of you. I will be your father."

No one could figure out why we had come to Balangao. They decided among themselves that perhaps we had plans to get rich. Some thought we might sell their language in America, since we were writing it down. Others guessed we were looking for husbands because we didn't have any.

We set about to learn to speak Balangao. We'd climb up the bamboo ladders into their smoky, dark, little one-roomed houses on stilts, sit by their open fires, eat rice and snails with our fingers and learn about why they sacrifice pigs and chickens to the evil spirits.

Daily we explained to our Balangao family about God, but no one listened to us. We were too young—"children"—and foreigners. However, God was at work in our Balangao father. In a dream he saw and asked a strange man, "Why have those American children come here?"

The man said, "They have come to tell you something that is more solid than a mighty rock. Believe what they tell you."

But in our first five years there only two believed. One man had told me, "We'd stop sacrificing pigs and chickens to the spirits if we just had protection, but what are we supposed to do if our children are sick? Let them die?"

Frustrated, we went back to America in 1967 for furlough. I was trained. I knew the answers. I tried to do all the right things. But only God can make people believe. I told my supporting churches of our frustrations. They prayed and then things began to change.

Upon returning to the Philippines in 1968, I gave my Balangao father a copy of First John that I had translated and asked him to "correct" the Balangao grammar. Before he finished reading it, he said, "My child, this is good! People would believe this if they could just hear it!"

I was amazed. I'd been trying to tell him that for six years! I asked, "What are we going to do so they can hear?" I didn't know it, but that was the wisest thing I'd ever said in Balangao—I asked him for help.

He went into the village and brought people to my house. Then he said to me, "Here we are, teach us." God was helping me follow the proper custom. Only when a father asks his daughter to teach can she speak, and then people will listen.

I told them how God himself had become a man to reach men and redeem them. They began to understand, because in a sense it was the same as their trying to redeem the lives of their children from the evil spirits.

After some months they asked, "What is it we tell God when we want to become his children?"

I gave them a simple prayer to pray. One man prayed right in the middle of our Bible study. Afterward he asked, "Is it OK if we tell this to other people?" The spirit of the evangelist!

Realizing I was responsible for the growth of these new believers, I started to translate the pastoral Epistles with my Balangao father—it seemed like the most logical thing to do for a new church. But I could not persuade these men to teach—even with my help. They insisted I do it all.

When we came to the verse in First Timothy where Paul says, "I don't allow women to teach men,"[3] my Balangao father didn't even make a comment. We just kept going.

That afternoon after we finished, he asked what we were studying on Sunday. I thought he was just curious, and I told him. On Sunday morning before I could stand and teach, he said, "My daughter here knows more about this than I do, but we found in the Bible where it says women aren't supposed to teach men, so I guess I'll have to." That's when the men started to teach in Balangao! What I could not do by reasoning power, God did by using his holy Word.

I realized more than ever that I needed to get the written Word into believers' hands as quickly as possible. Now the church in Balangao has grown and given birth to many other churches.

The work God has given me is difficult. But he doesn't call us to a life of ease. My work with the Balangaos is worth everything to me.

---

(1) Mark 16:15, KJV. (2) Cf. Matthew 28:19. (3) Cf. 1 Timothy 2:12

10
Proclaiming God's Word Today

"And he has committed to us the message of reconciliation. We are therefore Christ's ambassadors, as though God were making his appeal through us."
2 Corinthians 5:19-20, NIV

No "Coincidences" With God

John B. Aker

W hen I boarded a DC-10 one Monday morning at Newark International Airport, I was surprised to see that it was almost empty. The computer had decreed that I would sit beside a fellow-traveler, his was a window seat, mine the aisle. I looked across at the five empty seats in the middle of the plane and knew that as soon as the big bird lifted off, I intended to stretch out in them. But in the meantime, while we had those few moments, I thought I should be a bit sociable. So I began to speak to the passenger next to me.

His name was Richard. I learned shortly that we had some things in common. I had studied at the Army Intelligence School, so had he. I had married a woman who had served with Army Intelligence, he had also. I had three children, Richard did too. But that was where our commonalities ended.

As we got into our discussion, he told me that he had been to the Sloan-Kettering Institute for Cancer Research in New York Ci-

John B. Aker, D. Min., is senior pastor of Montvale Evangelical Free Church in Montvale, New Jersey, and was formerly vice president of Trinity College in Deerfield, Illinois. Dr. Aker and his wife, Rose, are the parents of three children. ©1986 John Aker.

ty. He had come to an agreement with his doctors that there would be no more chemotherapy, no more radiation treatment. He just wanted to go to his home in Nebraska where he worked as controller at a hospital. He wanted to live life full throttle. The doctors had told him it would be a matter of months—six, eight, ten—but not many.

As we continued our conversation, Richard turned toward me. Up until that point I had seen only the right side of his face. So normal, so whole. But now the left side came into view, little by little. And then I saw the ravages of his disease. "It is basal cell carcinoma," he said, "skin cancer." My father had had it, but on Richard it had run wild. For the first time I saw the way the tongue lay in the mouth, how the teeth bit up and down into the jaw, the way the eye socket is formed and holds the eye in place, because all that skin was gone. It was like one raw, open wound. I tried not to let that distract me as he continued his story.

Here was a man facing death, certain death—short of a special miracle from God. And his greatest concern was for those three children he was going to leave behind. He told me that he had been an only child, his wife also an only child. And then he sadly shared how, just a few months earlier, his wife had fallen down the steps on the way to the basement in their home. As a result of that fall, she had died. Now, as he faced the possibility of leaving his children, he knew that there were just his aged parents. They lived in Neptune, New Jersey, and hadn't really known anything outside that state. His children had never known anything apart from life in Nebraska. Death was so sure, the thought of leaving his children so somber. It was at that point I looked at him and asked, "Do you mind if I tell you about something that changed my life?"

As he nodded, I took the napkin that was left over from his breakfast and hastily sketched out the four spiritual laws. As I came to the end of that simple presentation, the cabin attendant suddenly interrupted our conversation with, "We are now preparing for final descent into Chicago-O'Hare International Airport."

With that I asked him, "Richard, will you trust Jesus Christ for your future—for what lies beyond the grave for you? Will you look to this One who left his own grave behind and believe that he holds hope for you and for the care of your children?"

Richard clutched my hand and said, "Pray with me." And right then, about 10,000 feet over the city of Chicago, Illinois, he gave his heart to Jesus Christ. We had just concluded the sinner's prayer when the plane touched down on the runway at O'Hare Airport. I remember walking down the ramp, following Richard out to the lobby. As we shook hands, I saw for a moment only that left side of his face, that portion that seemed dead. I felt burdened with the thoughts of the suffering, sorrow and final separation still before him. I turned for one last wave; and as I did, he was waving too. Now I saw the right side of his face—so fully alive, his warm smile visible. I reflected even then on the graciousness of our God who would take someone like me and allow me to share in his work, his miracle of taking men from death to life.

Had the story ended there, it would still remain so special. But within the next six weeks I relocated to Deerfield, Illinois, and assumed the responsibilities of vice president of Trinity College. Part of my duties included a great deal of traveling, representing that school to its founding denomination and speaking in churches, high schools and colleges across the country.

Several months later I was back on the East Coast preaching in the New York area. When I got on the plane the next Monday morning to fly from Newark to O'Hare Airport, I was tired but I was going home. I was seated next to an older woman. I didn't think she would mind if I just sat back, buckled up and went to sleep, so I did.

Shortly after breakfast had been served, I woke up and realized that I hadn't taken time to invest in her life, nor had I allowed her to share any of her life with me. I began our conversation by asking if she lived in Chicago. She told me she didn't. She was on her way to a little town in Nebraska. I asked her which town. She said, "Oh, you probably never heard of it."

I said, "Try me."

When she said the name of the town, I responded, "I know that town." She looked at me in total surprise. I said, "Yes, I sat with a man on this plane last November, this same flight." Then I told her his name.

She looked at me and said, "You must be John."

"How could you know that?" I asked.

Her reply was simply, "I'm Richard's mother." She went on to tell me how Richard was walking in that decision he had made for Christ. He was reading the Bible, getting together with his pastor almost weekly to pray and was concerned about Bible study. That delighted his mother's heart because she had known the Lord for a long time. It was special for her to have the assurance that Richard was taking these steps with the Lord.

But she told me too about her pain—how she had to stand by helplessly and watch her only son die. Then she almost echoed Richard's words as she expressed great concern about how she and her husband, who had never known anything outside New Jersey, would care for the children who had all their friends, all their roots, right there in Nebraska. What was she to do?

It was at that point that the cabin attendant announced, "We're now preparing for final descent into O'Hare Airport."

Our eyes locked as I said, "You know, this is when I prayed with Richard."

Just as her son had done, she took my hand and asked, "Would you pray with me?" And we prayed. We finished as the plane was pulling up to the ramp. She said, "I'm so encouraged."

"Encouraged," I said. "I feel inspired—to think that Richard has followed through on his decision, that he has been concerned about a deeper relationship with his Lord; to think about the way God takes our lives and puts all the pieces together so perfectly, just the way he arranged for us to sit together. People would never believe it."

Then she looked at me and said, "You know, this wasn't my seat. Just before you came on the plane a woman asked me to change seats with her."

◆ ◆ ◆

The gift has been given
The work has been done
The blood freely shed
The fight clearly won
The victory is ours, through
    God's risen Son!
    Christ has risen!
      Christ is Lord!
        Hallelujah! Amen!
    —LINDA C. CAIN
      Medfield, Massachusetts

Needed:
A Heaven-Sent Revival

Billy Graham

I once asked a university professor what he thought our greatest need was. He considered it carefully before answering. He said, "I could give you a variety of answers all the way from tax relief to disarmament. I may surprise you, because I'm not a religious man, but I believe that the greatest need that we have at this hour is a spiritual awakening which will restore individual and collective morals and integrity throughout the nation."

To bear the name "Christian" is not enough. We pride ourselves on being a "Christian" nation; but if our conduct doesn't measure up to Christian standards, condemnation will be ours: "Thou hast a name that thou livest, and art dead."[1]

To attend church is not enough. If we fail to let Christ be Lord and Master of our lives, we must come under the judgment of God, who said, "This people draweth nigh unto me with their mouth, and honoreth me with their lips; but their heart is far from me."[2]

It is easy to be carried along by a tide of religious enthusiasm without having a vital, personal experience with God. A hostile world is seething with hatred, intrigue, lawlessness and godless aggression. The wicked prosper, and in many areas of the world the righteous suffer. People are confused, unstable and unhappy. Scarcely, if ever, has economic prosperity been accompanied by such widespread unhappiness, lawlessness and rebellion.

The heart of the world is aching for peace, for reality and for God. The Prophet Habakkuk once stood in the midst of a people who had been showered with every conceivable blessing but who had lost their spiritual sanity, and he cried, "O Lord, revive thy work in the midst of the years."[3]

"But how," you may ask, "do we achieve renewal and revival? What are the steps to spiritual awakening?"

First, there must be earnest prayer. The Bible says, "If my people, which are called by my name, shall humble themselves, and pray, and seek my face, and turn from their wicked ways; then will I hear from heaven."[4] There must be a deep-seated heart-yearning for revival—not just a mere muttering of words, pious platitudes and religious mouthings, but earnest, fervent prayer. The Bible says, "The effectual fervent prayer of a righteous man availeth much."[5]

Let your soul be anguished; let the tears flow; let your heart be burdened for the lost. Tears are appropriate, for God's Word says, "He that goeth forth and weepeth, bearing precious seed, shall doubtless come again with rejoicing, bringing his sheaves with him."[6]

Second, we must forsake our sins. The Bible says, "Let the wicked forsake his way, and the unrighteous man his thoughts: and let him return unto the Lord."[7] Again the Bible says, "If my people shall forsake their wicked ways, then will I hear from heaven."[8]

The bickering, the prejudices, the ill will, the envy, the jealousy, the bitterness and the criticism among Christian people today must end before revival can begin. The world stands in awe at all the discord, strife and intolerance among us who profess Christ. The revival must begin in the hearts of Christians before evangelism can be effectively brought to the world.

When Christ's disciples settled their differences, gave up their selfishness, confessed their sins and allowed God's Spirit to fill them, revival came. We must forsake our evil ways. God's Spirit cannot operate in a climate of dissension and quarrels. We must forsake our pettiness, our peevishness, our littleness and our whims.

The enemy of souls has weakened the effectiveness of the Church because we have majored on controversy and dissension rather than on going forth weeping and bearing precious seed.[9] We have put much more emphasis on institutions than we have on prayer and on God.

May God forgive us and help us to forsake our wicked, contemptuous ways! If we are to have revival in our time, we must forsake our sins, individually and corporately as Christians.

Third, God must be real to us. The Bible says, "If my people shall seek my face, then will I hear from heaven."[8] In a world filled with crass materialism we have tried to whittle God down to our size. Our God seems to have become too small, and we are guilty of intellectual idolatry. We have created a god in our minds who is not the revealed God of the Bible.

We too often associate real, vital, personal Christian experience with people who are highly emotional. Many say, "It's all right to go to church, and a person ought to be decent, but I don't believe in going overboard on religion." They think the Christian faith is a phobia, bordering on mental incompetence.

If Christianity is important at all, it is all-important. If it is anything at all, it is everything. It is either the most vital thing in your life, or it isn't worth bothering with.

You can know God. Millions of Christians are saying with assurance, "I know I have passed from death unto life."[10] "I know whom I have believed."[11] We read in the Bible, "If any man will do his will, he shall know of the doctrine."[12]

We need a revival of Christian faith, of Christian experience, of God-consciousness. God has said, "If my people shall seek my face . . . "[8] If we will rediscover that he is holy, righteous, real, absolute and personal, and that he is a God of love and mercy, then this reality will be transferred to the world and revival can come. It has worked before in history. It will work again.

Don't give the lie to the Christian faith by professing Christ without possessing him. Don't lock the church door with the key of inconsistency and keep the lost from coming to Christ. Don't hinder revival by your unbelief and prayerlessness. Don't cheat yourself out of spiritual victory by allowing sin to imprison you. Seek God's face and turn from your wicked ways. Then you will hear from heaven.

The Church holds the key to revival. It is within our grasp. Will we rise to the challenge? Will we dare pay the price? The supply of heaven is adequate for the demands of our spiritually starved world. Will we fail to offer that supply?

Have you accepted Christ as your Savior? If you are honest, you will admit that deep down inside you is an emptiness that needs to be filled. Your heart yearns for peace and joy and forgiveness. There is a void that the earth cannot satisfy.

In the center of history on a low hill in Palestine a cross was erected—the cross of Christ, the Son of God. By some wonderful miracle known only to God, all who look to the Lamb slain on the cross have life—not just the good, the respectable and the decent—but the vile, the despicable and the outcast. A thief dying with Jesus looked believingly upon him and was assured of life everlasting.[13]

The Bible says, "Having made peace through the blood of his cross, by him to reconcile all things unto himself."[14]

Give your life to Christ today. And may the revival that the world needs begin in you.

---

(1) Revelation 3:1, KJV. (2) Matthew 15:8, KJV. (3) Habakkuk 3:2, KJV. (4) 2 Chronicles 7:14, KJV. (5) James 5:16, KJV. (6) Psalm 126:6, KJV. (7) Isaiah 55:7, KJV. (8) Cf. 2 Chronicles 7:14. (9) Psalm 126:6. (10) Cf. 1 John 3:14. (11) 2 Timothy 1:12, KJV. (12) John 7:17, KJV. (13) Luke 23:40-43. (14) Colossians 1:20, KJV

Before Awakening Can Begin

Charles W. Colson

T he Gospel is a two-edged sword. Jesus came not only to comfort the afflicted but to afflict the comfortable. Any hope for revival must begin with genuine repentance, our willingness to give up what we have and our desire to change.

The idea of losing our lives for his sake, as Christ tells his disciples to do, is not any more popular today, in our obsessively materialistic society, than it was to the rich young ruler (Luke 18:18-24).

Before any awakening can begin, I am convinced that we Christians must come to terms with some hard spiritual truths. Instead of "using" the Gospel to protect what we have, we need to come before our sovereign Master in repentance and surrender.

Revival is God's work; man cannot engineer it. But if we in good conscience ask our sovereign Creator to favor us with a mighty moving of his Spirit, we must obey his clear commands and never

Charles W. Colson is the founder and chairman of the board of Prison Fellowship, a Christian ministry to men and women in prison. A well-known author, speaker and columnist, he has written six books, including most recently "Kingdoms in Conflict." He and his wife, Patricia Ann, live near Washington, D.C. This excerpt was taken by permission from "Who Speaks for God?" by Charles Colson, ©1985 Charles Colson, Crossway Books, Westchester, Illinois.

distort his Gospel for our own self-seeking purposes.

The Gospel is Good News. But Jesus never said it was easy news. The central truth about the cross is death before life, repentance before reward. Before his Gospel can be the Good News of redemption, it must be the bad news of the conviction of sin.

"I Almost Ran Away From a Miracle"

Janice L. Hansen

H ow can I tell these girls how much Jesus loves them?" I wondered as I spread the frosting on Valentine cookies for my
Awana class. "I'll print 'Jesus loves you' in pure, white letters on
each cookie, personalizing them with each girl's name."

"Now," I thought, "if I only had a big gigantic heart I'd write
on it in huge letters, 'I love You, Jesus,' so all the world can see
how much I love him."

But my exclamations of love burst like a balloon, for I sensed
Jesus saying to me, "Do you really love Me, Jan?"

"Of course, I love You, Lord. I'm a Christian. I'm willing to serve
You. Why, I'm making these sugar cookies as a special treat for
my Awana girls to let them know that You love them and that I
love them too."

"If you love me, you will keep my commandments."*

"What commandments?" I asked.

I knew the answer.

My mind went back to a wintry January day several weeks before.

Janice L. Hansen is employed in a refrigeration plant in Greenville, Michigan,
and is also a free-lance writer of curriculum materials and radio scripts. She
attends Calvary Baptist Church. ©1981 Janice L. Hansen.

I had gotten up early that morning and arrived at the grocery store soon after it opened. When I was filling out my checkbook, a young woman pulled up her cart behind me.

"It's good to see you," she said. "How are you doing today?"

I looked up startled. Did I know her from somewhere? I didn't think so, but she surely acted as if I did.

"OK," I muttered. "How about you?"

"I'm tired," she replied. "I just got done working the third shift at the hospital. I don't usually shop in the mornings, but I'm out of everything. How about you?"

"Usually I shop on Mondays, but the weather changed my plans this week," I explained.

"Do you have a car?" she asked.

"Yes."

"I don't. I walked here. I live about six blocks away at the Winter Inn."

"That's not too far from my place," I said hesitantly, as I viewed her half-filled shopping cart.

I began to wheel my purchases away when she called after me: "Say, lady, can't you give me a ride home? I've got more than I can carry and I don't have the money for a cab."

Weakly I nodded. I knew I should have offered her a ride home in the first place.

As I dropped her off at the hotel, she told me her name was Diane and shoved a slip of paper into my mitten with her phone number on it. "Call me sometime so we can do something together, OK?" she asked.

I stuttered, "Sure, I will—sometime."

"Good, I'll be waiting for you to call," she said as she slammed the car door.

The rest of the way home I chided myself for getting into this predicament. Why couldn't I just have said, "No, I'm not interested," and been done with it all?

A couple of weeks passed, but I made no attempt to contact Diane. I thought of her whenever I passed the hotel, but I did nothing. It was never the right time.

Now it was more than a month later, and I still had done nothing. The smell of the cookies brought me back to the present.

"If you love me, you will keep my commandments."* I felt ashamed and guilty. Love was more than writing a message on a heart-shaped cookie. Love was an action word. I needed to demonstrate his love to others. I wanted to make cookies, but I wasn't willing to pass on his love. I laid down the frosting knife and went to dial Diane's number.

"I'm sorry, she's moved," the receptionist at the hotel said.

I sighed with relief. Maybe I had waited too long, but at least I had tried.

"Wait a minute," the receptionist continued. "I shouldn't do this, but I'll give you her forwarding address."

I scribbled the information down on my church bulletin. Now I had no excuse. I might as well go over there today.

I went over to Diane's apartment with some sugar cookies for her. She was surprised to see me; in fact, she didn't even know who I was. I faltered for words: "I, ah, gave you a ride home from the store in January, and, ah . . . "

"Yeah, so what?" she interrupted.

"I promised to call on you sometime, and here I am," I said with a laugh, trying to cover my nervousness.

"Oh, I remember you now," she said after a pause. "I just never thought I'd hear from you again."

"Well, I did promise," I almost apologized.

"Most people make promises that they never intend to keep," she said coolly. "Here, let me pick up some of the clothes on the couch to give you a place to sit," she mumbled. "I'm a sight today and slow to get around. I just got up an hour ago."

I glanced at the kitchen clock. It was after 3:00.

"We had a party last night. We really got high," she said, as she cleared some bottles off the table. "Do you want a joint?"

"No," I said in a hurry, and cried to myself: "What am I getting into, Lord? I don't belong here!"

"Why the cookies?" Diane asked.

"I, ah, made them for my Awana girls at church. Tomorrow is Valentine's Day," I said cautiously.

"Is that like Pioneer Girls?" she asked.

Her question caught me off guard. How did she know about such things?

"Well, is it?" she probed.

"Yes," I stammered, not knowing what else to say.

"I went to church when I was a teenager," Diane said. "Then I married young, ran off to New York, got into drugs and a lot of other things that I'm trying to forget and put behind me. These past four years have been a living hell." Then, softening her voice, she continued, "I promised God if I ever got back here I'd go to church again. God must have heard me—when I moved here, I found a church right next door."

"Have you gone to church?" I asked.

"No, I wanted to, really," she said. "I watched the people coming and going, but I couldn't go alone."

"Would you like to come to church with me?" I asked.

"Yes, I'd like that."

"How about tonight?" I asked with anticipation.

"No, I can't."

"But you said . . . "

"Listen, I will, but tonight—I already promised a girlfriend I'd go to her house for supper. Maybe next week."

I thought to myself, "Maybe next week, but probably not. Who is she kidding? I can tell a brushoff." I visited a while longer and then left. Now it was her turn to contact me.

The next week I was the surprised one. Diane kept her word. She went to church with me then and in the following weeks. After a few weeks she committed her life to the Lord, was baptized and joined the church.

Now Diane and I are close friends. Sometimes we laugh about the shaky way our friendship began. Then I think that if I had had my way, I would have run away from making a friend, run away from getting involved, run away from witnessing to God's love. I would have run away from a miracle.

---

*John 14:15, RSV

A Little Boy

Jeffrey A. Hatton

They moved into the apartment complex in November, a young mother, her five-year-old daughter and her two-year-old son. They took an upstairs apartment in the building.

One windy day in late November, as I approached this building to make my daily postal deliveries, I was greeted by the little girl and her brother; she was holding his hand. At once I was repulsed by the condition of the little boy's nose. It was draining in a solid mass from his nostrils to the top of his lips. "Maybe I should wipe it for him," I thought, but I had nothing to do it with.

The little girl asked my name and if they could go along with me. I told them who I was but that I preferred not to have them tagging along. They followed anyway. As we went along, I noticed that the little boy had no covering on his head. I turned to the little girl and said, "You had better get him inside; he has a cold."

"We can't get inside. Mommy left and the door is locked."

"You mean you can't get inside at all?" I asked. She shook her head "no."

Jeffrey A. Hatton is employed by the United States Postal Service. He and his wife, Janalyce, live in Indiana and are the parents of two children. They attend a Mennonite church. ©1982 Jeffrey A. Hatton.

"What about your daddy? Isn't he home?" I asked, thinking that surely one of the parents was home to watch them.

"Daddy don't live here."

"Then you better go to the office and have them give you another key so you can get inside," I told her. "Your brother needs to be out of this cold weather."

"We have an uncle who lives down the hall from us," she said. "We can get in there."

"Then you better go, and make sure your brother gets inside," I said with genuine concern for the little boy. They left, but they didn't go inside right away; a little later they were still wandering around outside their building.

I didn't see them again until a couple of weeks later. It was early December. I was surprised when the little girl remembered my name; as before, they wanted to follow me. This time neither of them had anything on their heads, and the little boy's nose was still a repulsive smear from nostrils to lip. Again I felt as if I should wipe it for him, but I had no handkerchief.

"Pull your hood up over your head," I said to the little girl as we walked along. "And he needs something on his head too. He's going to get pneumonia."

"He had pneumonia last week. He was in the hospital," she said, as she pulled the hood on her coat over her head.

A couple of weeks passed without any sign of the children. Then one day, near the end of the year, as I approached their building, I heard someone hollering my name. Looking up, I saw those two little kids sitting in the window of their apartment, the girl up high and the boy down low. The window was an aluminum sliding unit, and they had pulled back the glass pane so that only the screen portion was between them and the late December weather. They wanted to talk to me, but I just said, "Hi," and continued on my way. The same thing happened another time or two, but I never stopped to talk.

One morning early in January, as I reported for work, a fellow worker asked if I had heard about the fire in the apartment complex the previous night. I hadn't. "There was one confirmed death," he said.

That afternoon at the complex I discovered the awful truth for myself. The little boy with the smeary nose was dead. I learned that the mother had been preparing food on the kitchen stove at two o'clock in the morning. Needing an ingredient, she left the apartment with the food still cooking on the stove and had gone down the hall to the uncle's apartment to see if he had what she needed. Whatever was on the stove had become too hot and started a fire. By the time it was discovered, the apartment was too hot to enter. Fire officials found the little boy's body lying on the floor of his bedroom, amid his toys. The little girl had been staying with relatives that night or she too might have perished.

So the little boy passed from the scene. His needs had been few. Just a little more attention from the people who made up his world could have seen him through. And now, in retrospect, I find myself saying, "If only I had it to do over again, how differently I would do it."

If it is true that a sparrow cannot fall out of his nest to the ground and escape God's notice, if common lilies of the field are clothed with the robes of kings and fowls of the air are fed from God's attentive care, then surely God also cared about that little boy.

But I hadn't cared.

Jesus said, "Suffer the little children to come unto me, . . . for of such is the kingdom of God," but I hadn't invited that little boy into my life.

I should have done more.

Insistent

John R. Corts

John R. Corts, program director for Amsterdam '86, also handled the follow up for Amsterdam '83. He tells the following experience.—ED.

O ne of the first projects we faced in 1983 was a request by a Filipino evangelist who wanted 100,000 New Testaments. He was insistent. "I must have them, and I must have them within the next six months."

So I asked, "Why do you need 100,000?"

"Because," he said, "I can distribute 100,000 in the Philippines in the next six months."

I challenged that, so I wrote to some of the references he had given me and asked, "Do you think that it is realistic for this man to ask for 100,000 New Testaments?"

The answer came back, "It is absolutely realistic."

Now I was a little curious about that because that's a lot of literature. So I wrote again to the person who was giving approval and asked, "What makes you so positive that this man can do it?"

He came right back with his answer: "Because he already did it in the last six months."

John R. Corts is chief operating officer and vice president of operations at the Billy Graham Evangelistic Association in Minneapolis, Minnesota. He and his wife, Jo-Ann, are the parents of a daughter and live in Eden Prairie. ©1987 Billy Graham Evangelistic Association.

So I wrote once more to the evangelist and asked, "Sir, how would you carry 100,000 New Testaments? That's a lot of literature. You surely need a bicycle, a motor bike, an automobile—a van?"

"No," he wrote, "I just carry them on my back."

Again I wrote asking other questions, and I wrote to some other people to see what kind of ministry this man had, and what his church relationship was.

Finally one man wrote to me and said, "Sir, you've written a number of letters, and already a couple of months have gone by. Don't you understand it is urgent that this man get those 100,000 New Testaments?"

I replied, "What's so urgent about it?"

He responded, "Because he has a terminal cancer."

Then I asked the question, "How old is this man?"

He answered, "Eighty-one years of age."

Imagine—81 years old with terminal cancer, and his request had been so urgent because he had been told he had six months to live.

"Give me 100,000 New Testaments. I can carry them on my back. I'll distribute them in the next six months."

"How do you know?"

"Because I just did it."

Then I asked myself a question: "How many New Testaments have I given out with two good legs and a few years to go before I'm 81?"

11
Remembering God's Saving Work Today

"Worthy is the Lamb, who was slain, to receive power and wealth
and wisdom and strength and honor and glory and praise!"
Revelation 5:12, NIV

The Peace of Christmas

Billy Graham

I t was Christmastime, 1818, in Oberndorf, a little town in the beautiful Austrian Alps, and the Reverend Josef Mohr, the 26-year-old assistant pastor of St. Nicholas Church, wrote a poem celebrating the glory of the birth of Jesus Christ. Mohr brought the poem to Franz Grüber, the church organist, and requested that the musician set the words to music. That night, Christmas Eve, Grüber and Mohr sang their melody accompanied by guitar, little dreaming that this song would go around the world and become possibly the greatest Christmas carol of them all—"Silent Night! Holy Night!"

But in much of the world today the night is not silent, and it is not holy. For ours is a world of political, economic, and social turmoil. If there is one word that seems to describe the mood of people in our world today, it is the word "fear." It seems as though every day the newspaper headlines scream of some new crisis in our world that threatens to plunge us into chaos.

Just as real and just as tragic are the personal crises that don't make the headlines—the marriage that is falling apart, the heart-ache of a broken relationship, the despair of a lost job, the threat of illness, the slavery of a drug or an alcohol problem that seems unbreakable.

Jesus spoke of a time when "men's hearts would fail them for fear."[1] We seem to be living in just such a time as that today. "Silent Night! Holy Night!" seems like a romantic dream or even a false hope that vanishes in the face of the realities of life. But there can be peace in our hearts when we turn to the only true source of peace, Jesus Christ.

Think back to that first Christmas almost 2,000 years ago. The stars shone like diamonds in the sky, and the little band of weary shepherds had settled down to sleep on the cold, rocky ground outside the little village of Bethlehem.

They had no reason to expect that this night would be different from any other, just as you may think that nothing can change in your life. But God had other plans. This was the night when God himself would come to earth.

Read Luke's account of that remarkable night: "And, lo, the angel of the Lord came upon them, and the glory of the Lord shone round about them: and they were sore afraid. And the angel said unto them, Fear not: for, behold, I bring you good tidings of great joy, which shall be to all people. For unto you is born this day in the city of David a Savior, which is Christ the Lord."[2]

Can you imagine the fear that must have gripped their hearts? One translation says, "And they were terror-stricken."[3]

But the first words of the angel to those shepherds were, "Fear not." Four times in the Gospel accounts of Christmas the angels used that expression, "Fear not."

Zacharias, an old man, was filled with fear when an angel appeared. He was told that he would be a father and that his son would be the forerunner of the Messiah. The angel told him, "Fear not."[4]

Mary was told that she would have the awesome privilege of bearing the Son of God. Fear filled her at first, but the angel said, "Fear not, Mary."[5]

Joseph, betrothed to Mary, was filled with fear and embarrassment when he learned that she was pregnant. But the angel declared, "Fear not . . . : for that which is conceived in her is of the Holy Ghost."[6]

Then when the Holy Child was born, the angel came to those shepherds in the fields and said, "Fear not: for, behold, I bring you good tidings of great joy. . . . For unto you is born . . . a Savior, which is Christ the Lord."[7]

And that is what God says to us today, no matter what our fears may be. It is what he is saying to you right now—"Fear not." Fear not, because Christ has come.

The angels tell us to "fear not." Why? Because we no longer have any reason to be gripped and enslaved by fear. Think of the fears that so easily assault us.

There is the fear of problems that we face and what we think they may do to us. But no matter what problem we face, the Bible says, "Fear not." Why? Because Christ is with us. Jesus declared, "In the world ye shall have tribulation: but be of good cheer; I have overcome the world."[8]

He invites you to bring your cares and your burdens to him. He said, "Come unto me, all ye that labor and are heavy laden, and I will give you rest."[9]

And there is the fear of loneliness. We are never alone when we know Christ. He has promised, "Lo, I am with you [always], even unto the end of the world."[10] We were created for fellowship with God; and when we come to Christ, he makes us a child of God. We have a special relationship with him, and nothing can take that away, because Christ made it possible through his death on the cross.

Then there is the fear of death. There was another time in the Bible when the angel came and said, "Fear not."[11] It was spoken to the women who came to the tomb of Jesus early on that first Easter morning and discovered that the tomb was empty. "Fear not ye. . . . He is not here: for he is risen."[12]

Christ is the answer to death. By his death on the cross and his resurrection from the dead, he took away the sting of death.[13] He took away our sins by dying on the cross in our place. And by putting our faith in him as Lord and Savior, we can know the joy of forgiveness and peace with God.

Christmas was just the beginning. Ahead was the cross. And beyond the cross was the empty tomb. Christ has come to take away the source of our fears. When we realize that he has dealt with sin and made it possible for us to be reconciled to God, then we do not need to be paralyzed by fear any longer. We can come to Christ with our sins and cast them at his feet.

We can know "Silent Night! Holy Night!" in our hearts. We can know what the Bible calls "the peace of God, which passeth all understanding."[14] Jesus promised, "Peace I leave with you, my peace I give unto you: not as the world giveth, give I unto you. Let not your heart be troubled, neither let it be afraid."[15]

Christmas emphasizes the glorious truth that what man is unable to do for himself, Jesus Christ has done for him. Man cannot save himself, because he cannot deliver himself from the guilt, power and consequences of sin. Man is in rebellion against God and has no terms of peace to offer that are acceptable to God. Only God himself can make peace, and this he did through the atoning sacrifice of his Son. Through the merits of Christ's life and death, we are offered full and free forgiveness.

To know the pardon, joy, peace and power which come through Christ, we must personally receive him by faith. Faith must be real if the heart is to be changed. You too can find the peace for which you have searched so long.

You ask, "What do I have to do?" You have to turn from your sins and receive Christ as your Lord and Savior; commit your life to him.

He will come into your heart, and this Christmas you can know the Christ of Christmas. Whatever your need, Jesus can meet that need. Christ can touch your life and transform you and make you a new person. Make the heart commitment to Jesus Christ. He will receive you, and he can transform your life.

---

(1) Cf. Luke 21:26. (2) Luke 2:9-11, KJV. (3) Luke 2:9, Phillips; taken by permission from the New Testament in Modern English, Revised Edition , tr. by J. B. Phillips. ©1958, 1960, 1972 J. B. Phillips, Macmillan Publishing Company, New York: Collins Publishers, London, England. (4) Luke 1:13, KJV. (5) Luke 1:30, KJV. (6) Matthew 1:20, KJV. (7) Luke 2:10-11, KJV. (8) John 16:33, KJV. (9) Matthew 11:28, KJV. (10) Matthew 28:20, KJV. (11) Matthew 28:5, KJV. (12) Matthew 28:5-6, KJV. (13) 1 Corinthians 15:55. (14) Philippians 4:7, KJV. (15) John 14:27, KJV

Christmas Day in Prison

George Miller

Merry Christmas, Mom. Maybe I will be home next year," said an inmate. "I'm sorry I can't be there with you this year."

These words are applicable to almost everyone in prison calling home for the holidays. But many don't have a home to call.

Christmas is a lonely time for most prisoners. To some it is just another "God-cursed" day.

No presents are opened around the three-foot evergreen loaded with Christmas lights, a garland and an oversized golden star. Its view is limited to most of the inmates from inside their locked buildings. One gets only a passing glimpse of the tree as he goes from one supervised area to another.

The big event is a concert put on by a group of talented inmates. Instead of "O Come, All Ye Faithful," or "Silent Night! Holy Night!" or "Hark! The Herald Angels Sing," they perform rock 'n' roll songs written by fellow inmates. Christ isn't even mentioned. The rest of the day is lost to the television set.

George Miller is a clerk for Pride Dental Lab at the Union Correctional Institution in Raiford, Florida. Mr. Miller attends All Souls Chapel (Pentecostal) at the Union Correctional Institution. ©1987 George Lee Miller.

Spirits aren't too high. Some prisoners are filled with hatred for themselves as well as for everyone else.

"Merry Christmas," shouted Mac to Lee.

"Well, it's Christmas, but I don't know about the merry part," snapped Lee.

All of this isn't a pretty picture, but it is reality. The attitude of many inmates is: "Where is Christ throughout this day? Where are those to whom Jesus said, 'I was in prison, and ye came unto me'?* Is even a small prayer prayed for me?"

"I can't believe that another year has come and gone and my family hasn't written me," said Tom. "I haven't received a visit or any Christmas cards from them."

With some inmates, their family dissociates from them while they are in prison. "I'll help you in any way I can as long as you are not in prison." This is a heartbreaking statement to hear.

But a few other prisoners are having a merry Christmas. They are worshiping God and singing praises to him in spite of their incarceration. Their hearts are free.

Some inmates walk from cell to cell greeting each other.

"Merry Christmas, George. You are like a brother to me," said Curtis.

"Thanks, I appreciate you too," I replied. "Merry Christmas."

---

*Matthew 25:36, KJV

When faith grows into full assurance so that we are certain beyond a doubt that the blood of Jesus has washed us whiter than snow, it is then that repentance reaches to its greatest height. Repentance grows as faith grows. Do not make any mistake about it; repentance is not a thing of days and weeks, a temporary penance to be got over as fast as possible! No, it is the grace of a lifetime, like faith itself. Repentance is the inseparable companion of faith.

—C. H. SPURGEON

From "All of Grace," by C. H. Spurgeon, Moody Press, Chicago, Illinois

Death Is Conquered

Billy Graham

Throughout the Christian world we are celebrating the most triumphant day in world history. Easter makes Christianity unique and sets it apart from all other world religions. Its distinction is that it has a living Lord.

The resurrection has been attested to in the greatest book ever written, the Bible. The Apostle Paul said, "Christ died for our sins according to the scriptures; And that he was buried, and that he rose again the third day according to the scriptures: And that he was seen of Cephas, then of the twelve: After that, he was seen of above five hundred brethren at once; . . . After that, he was seen of James; then of all the apostles. And last of all he was seen of me also."[1]

The bodily resurrection of Christ is not something which we can prove to unbelievers by logic or rationalization. Knowledge on the higher level is most often gained not by abstract argument but by personal experience. For example, falling in love can best be understood when you become a partaker of that experience. Just so, those who have been made partakers of the resurrection of Christ are positively assured of the veracity of the great truth that Christ rose bodily from the dead.

As Easter bells in churches and cathedrals around the world sound, not the death knell of Christ but the victorious chime of the living Lord, those glad words, "He is risen," come freshly to believing hearts everywhere. To those who have never known him and the power of his resurrection the Easter bells have no significance. But the company of believers who know their significance, along with those first few who gathered in the Easter garden, shout with exultant voices, "The Lord is risen indeed!"

During Napoleon's Austrian campaign his army advanced to within six miles of Feldkirch. It looked as though Bonaparte's men would take Feldkirch without resistance. But as Napoleon's army advanced toward their objective in the night, the Christians of Feldkirch gathered in a little church to pray. It was Easter eve.

The next morning at sunrise the bells of the village pealed out across the countryside. Napoleon's army, not realizing it was Easter Sunday, thought that in the night the Austrian army had moved into Feldkirch and that the bells were ringing in jubilation. Napoleon ordered a retreat, and the battle at Feldkirch never took place. The Easter bells caused the enemy to retreat, and peace reigned in the Austrian countryside.

At this Eastertime many of you are surrounded by enemies which storm the citadel of your soul. The Easter bells, when you realize their full significance, cause the threatening forces to retreat.

Before the resurrection the disciples were disillusioned. Peter denied Christ, Judas betrayed him and the rest forsook him. The disciples were besieged by doubts, fears, frustrations and anxiety. Cowed, they hid behind closed doors, afraid to face their friends with the awfulness of Golgotha in the minds of everyone, afraid to face the angry rabble who had killed their leader lest a like fate be theirs, afraid to face the future with its broken hopes and shattered dreams, afraid to face themselves and the reality of their own disillusionment. Had the world ever seen such a pitiful, dejected and disconcerted group of people?

Then it happened! Like a blast of trumpets at sunrise after a night of unthinkable horror, came the cry and the proclamation, "He is risen!" From street to street, from house to house, the message came, "The Lord is risen indeed!" What did it mean? What significance did it hold for the disciples? What bearing did it have on the future of Christianity?

First, the resurrection dispelled all doubts. Those who had not made contact with the living Lord, those who did not know him and the power of his resurrection naturally had doubts. Remember Thomas? That Christ should have risen was inconceivable to him:

"Except I shall see in his hands the print of the nails, . . . I will not believe."[2]

How did Thomas triumph over his doubts? He did not do it by speculation but by a revelation. Jesus appeared to him and said, "Reach hither thy finger, and behold my hands ; . . . and be not faithless, but believing."[3] It was in the sublimity of that personal relationship with the living Lord that Thomas said, "My Lord and my God."[4] Belief comes when you enter into an intimate, personal relationship with the Christ of Easter. To stand in the presence of a resurrected glorified Savior, resplendent with the radiance of another world, is to repeat the word of that believing disciple: "My Lord and my God"![4]

Second, the resurrection dissipated fear. The Bible says, "And if Christ be not raised, your faith is vain."[5] Faith cannot exist in dead, lifeless matter. All of the hopes of that little band of believers were locked up in the tomb of Joseph of Arimathea with the linen-wrapped body of their Lord. Implicit faith had given way to stark fear. The Bible says, "The doors were shut where the disciples were assembled for fear."[6]

We live in a world which is shaken by fear, apprehension and anxiety. The farther we get from the fact of the resurrection, the closer we get to the fear of destruction. The words "Christ or chaos" have come to be more than clever alliteration. They express an alternative which we must act upon.

Individuals are locked in prisons of fear. Nations tremble in the grip of collective fear. Cities are held in the dire clutch of fear. What is the answer to this stifling fear which is in the world?

The fear of those first disciples disappeared when they found themselves in the presence of their living Lord. The words, "Be not afraid,"[7] will dispel fear in any century. The answer to individual fear is a personal faith in a living, glorified Lord.

And the answer to collective fear is a corporate faith in a living, glorified Lord. The answer to national and international tensions and fears is for the world to know him who is alive forevermore. We do not worship a dead Christ. We worship a risen Christ! He is living today! And the Bible says that he is sitting at the right hand of God the Father. The Bible further teaches that this living Christ is coming personally to this earth again someday. The Church has hope today because of the resurrected Christ.

Third, the resurrection meant that death's decree had been broken. The Bible says, "For as in Adam all die, even so in Christ shall

all be made alive."[8] For centuries death had held mankind in its viselike grip. But around the opened door of Christ's empty tomb bloomed the lilies of immortality. The words "Because I live, ye shall live also"[9] negated death's decree and opened the gates of a blissful eternity for everyone who is clothed in the garments of everlasting life through faith in his name.

Paul sang triumphantly, "O death, where is thy sting? O grave, where is thy victory?"[10] We are told that many of the disciples paid the supreme sacrifice upon the altar of devotion for the love of their Lord. Fresh in their minds were the words of their Savior: "I am the resurrection, and the life: he that believeth in me, though he were dead, yet shall he live."[11]

Fourth, the resurrection is the answer to loneliness. Some of you are suffocated by a depressing loneliness. But God did not create you to live in unbearable solitude. God was the first to realize that it is not good for us to live alone. Christ, through his life, death and resurrection, provided an effective cure for the inherent loneliness of mankind. Not only to the disciples but to everyone of every age he said, "Lo, I am with you alway, even unto the end of the world."[12] He came to restore the lost fellowship of God and to bridge forever the gap of human loneliness.

The two disciples who walked sadly along the Emmaus road were symbolic of all of the lonely people who have never known the living Lord. Jesus said, "What manner of communications are these that ye have one to another, as ye walk, and are sad?"[13] But after they had touched him personally and experienced the power of his presence, they asked, "Did not our heart burn within us, while he talked with us by the way, and while he opened to us the scriptures?"[14] Their loneliness was dispelled by the resurrected Christ.

Earth has no balm that can cure the loneliness of the human spirit. Our souls cry out for fellowship with God, and Christ alone can fill this longing of our hearts.

When D. L. Moody asked Andrew Bonar, of Scotland, the secret of his power, he replied, "For 50 years I have had access to the throne of grace." Yes, a resurrected Christ is accessible. No one needs to be out of touch with the risen Christ. He is sitting at the right hand of God, the Father. And you have access to the throne of grace.

Fifth, the resurrection means that we are not in our sins anymore. The Bible says, "If Christ be not raised, your faith is vain; ye are yet in your sins."[15] Paul, who wrote those words, had declared, "Ye are washed, but ye are sanctified, but ye are justified in the name of the Lord Jesus, and by the Spirit of our God."[16] Again and again he made statements like this: "There is therefore now no condemnation to them which are in Christ Jesus."[17]

I tell you this with all the authority of the Word of God that every person who puts his trust in Christ can become a partaker of eternal life. When we do, the moment we die our soul goes into eternity to live with Christ forever. The Bible says that someday the bodies of the dead in Christ shall rise, and we shall ever be with the Lord.

Because Jesus was raised from the dead, our loneliness is conquered, our fears dispelled and our sins forgiven; we are on our way to heaven. We have access to God in Christ.

Today give him your life. Trust him as your Savior. Surrender your will to him; know the thrill and the joy and the security of the resurrected Christ living in you.

---

(1) 1 Corinthians 15:3-8, KJV. (2) John 20:25, KJV. (3) John 20:27, KJV. (4) John 20:28, KJV. (5) 1 Corinthians 15:17, KJV. (6) John 20:19, KJV. (7) Matthew 28:10, KJV. (8) 1 Corinthians 15:22, KJV. (9) John 14:19, KJV. (10) 1 Corinthians 15:55, KJV. (11) John 11:25, KJV. (12) Matthew 28:20, KJV. (13) Luke 24:17, KJV. (14) Luke 24:32, KJV. (15) 1 Corinthians 15:17, KJV. (16) 1 Corinthians 6:11, KJV. (17) Romans 8:1, KJV

"I Had No Idea!"

Blanche H. Gallup

I t was Holy Week. As chairman of the altar committee, I was asked to decorate the altar for the Good Friday treore service. It is my belief that the altar arrangement is an integral part of the service and should set the mood. As the congregation is seated, what they see prepares their thoughts for the service which follows.

We see Good Friday in the triumphant light of the resurrection. It was not "Good Friday" to the early Christians. They had only the sorrow and loss of Jesus at the crucifixion without the joy and comfort of the resurrection. For them it was a time of fear, failure and futility. I wanted to depict this view of the Friday before the resurrection.

With this in mind I felt that the richly embellished, shiny golden cross was far too ornate for the Good Friday that I wished to portray. As I read the story of the crucifixion, one sentence kept echoing in my mind: "They made a crown of thorns." It was the answer to my assignment. I would make a crown of thorns to lay on the altar.

Blanche H. Gallup (1895-1983) was a wedding consultant and worked in retail sales for a Christmas card company. She lived in Ann Arbor, Michigan, and attended First United Methodist Church. ©1981 Blanche H. Gallup.

I had never seen a crown of thorns, except in religious art, and had never expected to make one.

There was a black locust hedge across the road from our house. The limbs were low and full of thorns. It seemed it would not be difficult to get a few branches to make the crown. With a pair of clippers I tried to cut off a twig, and soon found that it was not going to be easy. The sharp, pointed thorns pricked my fingers and scratched my hands. In a short time they were sore and bleeding. I took a few branches home and tried to braid them into a circle. This was even more difficult. The stiletto-sharp thorns dug deep into my flesh. I put on leather gloves. The thorns went through the leather as though it were butter. I then tried workmen's heavy, rubber gloves. They were no better. Finally I took two pairs of pliers and tried to bend the branches into place.

As I worked, my thoughts wandered. Who made the crown of thorns? What kind of person was he? Whoever he was, certainly he had torn, bleeding hands for his effort. As I tried to visualize the event, I seemed to become a part of the faceless humanity being swept along the road to Calvary. The people in the mob impatiently pushed and jostled one another for position. It was a hot, sultry day. The air, so heavy and still, was hard to breathe. Long, flowing robes billowed and flapped against sticky ankles. Small puffs of dust, kicked up by shuffling sandals, blew across the road. Children clinging to nervous, frightened, weeping women were pushed and swept along with the throng. The staccato yipping of a mongrel dog, darting in and out through the crowd, added to the turmoil. A constant, low, rumbling roar of voices, punctuated by angry shouts of "Crucify him! Crucify him!" rose above the din. Love, hate, compassion and violence intermingled along the road to Golgotha.

Now and then the crowd parted, and I caught a glimpse of Jesus, plodding along, staggering and falling under the weight of the heavy cross. A crown of thorns was on his head. Blood streamed down his tortured face.

Again I questioned, "Who made that crown of thorns?" There was no answer except that ambiguous word "They." Yet I knew that someone in that jeering mob had made it. Someone with bleeding hands.

The crown I was making was finished, and I quit daydreaming. I looked at my bleeding hands and what they had made. My hands, which for 13 years had made hundreds of beautiful floral arrangements for the altar at the church, had just made one of the most diabolical symbols of cruelty and torture that I could imagine.

Later, at the church, I built up the center of the altar and draped it with royal purple velvet. I placed the crown of thorns on top, displaying it as a royal diadem might be exhibited for all to see. One long, daggerlike thorn in front dug deep into the velvet. It was an awesome sight.

The minister came in. He stood there in deep thought. Then silently he picked up the crown and gingerly placed it on his head. After carefully laying it back on the altar, he said, "I just wanted to see how it felt."

When the Good Friday service was over, many people went forward for a close view of the crown of thorns. I stood on the outer edge of the crowd to see and hear their reactions. I saw on their faces the anguish and distress that I had felt. I heard the embarrassed coughs to cover up the strain and torment they were feeling. Several persons quickly wiped tears from their eyes. Some wept openly and unashamedly, oblivious of others around them.

As one man left, I heard him murmur, "I had no idea! I had no idea!"

When we come to a full awareness of the fact of God's total and unchanging love for us, we cannot remain the same people we used to be. We naturally want to return that love, to repay it. This is part of God's plan, that our lives should make his love evident in our world. When we know in the depth of our being that we are loved, we are freed to love others. And in so doing we become more like God himself.

    —JOYCE DONALDSON MINOR